CW01666906

Essentials of

Yoga Practice and Philosophy

Text and compilation by

Swami Sitaramananda

SIVANANDA YOGA VEDANTA CENTER

This booklet is dedicated to all sincere spiritual seekers and serious Yoga practitioners around the world, in commemoration of the 50th Anniversary (1957–2007) of Swami Vishnu-devananda spreading the message of Yoga and Vedanta in the West.

© 2007, 2010, 2018 Sivananda Yoga Vedanta Center

Published by Swami Sitaramananda for Sivananda Yoga Vedanta Center

Foreword

The Sivananda teaching is a traditional Yogic teaching coming through a lineage of Yoga Masters, including Swami Sivananda and Swami Vishnu-devananda.

Master Sivananda's approach to Yoga, the synthesis of Yoga, is well-rounded and practical, written in almost 300 books.

Swami Vishnu-devananda, founder of the International Sivananda Yoga Vedanta Centers, taught students in both the East and West, giving innumerable lectures and writing two bestselling books: *The Complete Illustrated Book of Yoga* and *Meditation and Mantras*. His teachings are practical, humorous, and well-suited to modern Western lifestyles.

The "Essentials of Yoga Practice and Philosophy" is a summary of the core teachings of these two Masters presented in a nutshell. It is a helpful introduction to beginners or for first-time visitors to Sivananda Ashrams and Centers.

Om Shanti

Table of Contents

SWAMI SIVANANDA AND SWAMI VISHNU-DEVANANDA, RISHIKESH, HIMALAYAS

CHAPTER 1

The Masters

"Serve, Love, Give, Purify, Meditate, Realize."

– Swami Sivananda

SWAMI SIVANANDA (1887–1963) was born in South India to a pious Brahmin family. He became a medical doctor and hospital director during his pre-sannyas life in Malaysia. He found out that curing people of their physical ailments did not really solve the problem of human suffering and he started his quest to find the answer, becoming a wandering sadhu and starting to practice intense tapas (austerities) and meditation in Rishikesh, Himalayas. He became not only a doctor of the body but also a "doctor of the soul". He founded the Sivananda ashram in 1932 and the Divine Life Society in 1936 and published 200-300 books in English outlining practices for a spiritual life.

His teachings can be summarized in six words: "Serve, Love, Give, Purify, Meditate, Realize". He attained Mahasamadhi in 1963. The government of India published a stamp in his honor for his 100 year birthday anniversary, as he is recognized as an authoritative teacher in classical Yoga. Swami Sivananda, foreseeing that the whole world would need Yoga teachings, wrote his books in English, accepted western disciples, and sent some of his closest disciples to the West to teach Yoga. One of his foremost disciples is Swami Vishnu-devananda, whom he sent to America in 1957 with the words: "Go to America, people are waiting."

SWAMI VISHNU-DEVANANDA

SWAMI VISHNU-DEVANANDA (1927–1993) was born in Kerala, South India, and took sanniyas under Swami Sivananda at age 21. Master Sivananda nominated him as "Hatha Yoga Professor" at an early age, recognizing his extraordinary talents in this field. Swami Vishnu-devananda stayed with his Master in Rishikesh for 10 years before he was sent to America in 1957 to spread the teachings of Yoga and Vedanta to the masses. He was a pioneer in teaching the Yogic Lifestyle of the five points, and introduced the West to the concept of Yoga Vacations, Yoga Teachers Training courses, and Yoga Children's camp.

His approach was classical yet practical, adapted to modern needs and lifestyles. He is the author of the best-selling *Complete Illustrated Book of Yoga*, translated into more than a dozen languages around the world. He also authored *Meditation and Mantras* and wrote a commentary to Swami Swatmarama's *Hatha Yoga Pradipika*. Swamiji founded the International Sivananda Yoga Vedanta Centers with a dozen ashrams and 30 to 40 centers around the world. In 1969 he also founded the True World Order to train new leaders in inner Peace. Thus Swamiji, and the Sivananda organization, have trained 20,000 Yoga teachers around the world and continue to reach out to millions. Swamiji was also a world renowned Peace missionary, famous for his dangerous peace missions and flights around the world to where actual conflicts were taking place, such as the Suez Canal, Belfast, Pakistan, Berlin Wall, etc. Swamiji tirelessly brought to mankind the message of "Unity in Diversity" and "Health is wealth, peace of mind is happiness, and Yoga shows the way." He attained Mahasamadhi in 1993 in India.

The International Sivananda Organization has actively carried on his teaching mission in many countries, with worldwide Teachers Training Courses and by publishing books such as *The Sivananda Companion to Yoga*, and *Yoga, Mind, & Body*.

This booklet is a summary of the teachings of these two Masters, the essential teachings of Yoga philosophy and practice from the Sivananda lineage.

SWAMI VISHNU-DEVANANDA

CHAPTER 2

Satsanga and Meditation

"Satsang or the company of the wise removes the darkness and impurities of the heart, leads one to the divine path and causes the divine light to shine in one's heart."

– Swami Sivananda in *Elixir Divine*

WHY DO WE NEED SATSANGA?

Our normal thinking (concerning material and worldly things such as money, family, etc.) is very mundane. We rarely have time for deep contemplation, to renew our spiritual connection or to meditate on our life choices. Satsang, or company of the wise, through listening to lectures, reading books of Masters, and being in their presence, helps to induce in our mind inspiring and enlightening thoughts which can uplift and change our thinking, creating positive thoughts and inspiration in our minds. These beneficial influences and teachings can come through books, scriptures or, best, through live teachings.

Format of the Sivananda Satsang: Swami Sivananda's method of teaching is "Little...little". He doesn't recommend doing too much of the same practice, thus avoiding the egoism which comes with specialization, but recommends doing a little bit of each practice all day long, promoting well-rounded development and avoiding extremes. This practice also allows you to use your time for sadhana most effectively. Thus the mind is not saturated and receives a variety of different energies to keep it at a high and positive wavelength.

The format of satsang followed by the International Sivananda organization is the same format of satsang taught by Swami Sivananda in Rishikesh.

It is composed of:

30 minutes of silent meditation
30 minutes of kirtan (devotional chanting)
30 minutes of lecture or inspirational reading from the Masters' books
This is followed by concluding prayers and Arati (a light ceremony)

In the International Sivananda Ashrams and Centers, we read from the teachings of Master Sivananda and Swami Vishnu-devananda. Oftentimes, one of his disciples who has imbibed the teachings will give a discourse on a particular topic of Yoga philosophy and practice. Spiritual teaching is a matter of Guruparampara (transmission through a lineage of teachers and disciples) and therefore it is the norm that the teachings of the Masters are highlighted, and the present and living teacher acts only as their instrument. By following this spiritual discipline, we preserve the purity of the teaching and avoid personality worship which can corrupt the teachings of the Masters.

INTRODUCTION TO MEDITATION: BASIC TECHNIQUES

In classical Yoga, the practice of Yoga is linked intimately with the practice of meditation. "Meditation is the only royal road to the attainment of Freedom. It is a mysterious ladder which reaches from earth to heaven, from error to truth, from darkness to light, from pain to bliss, from restlessness to abiding peace, from ignorance to knowledge, from mortality to immortality", according to Sivananda in *Bliss Divine*.

One needs to resort to meditation to find answers in life, as our mind always leads us to frustration and makes us experience over and over again the same difficulties. It is only through meditation that we can shift our mind into new, helpful grooves, change ourselves deeply, and be aware of the present and our choices, rather than just living conditioned by the past or in an illusive pursuit of the future. Meditation gives us intuitional insights and connects us with a reality and a peace beyond the reach of speech and mind. That reality is our own True Self,

Sat-Chit-Ananda (Existence, Knowledge and Bliss Absolute), which is deeply fulfilling, holding the keys to all answers, without which we will feel empty and purposeless. Meditation is universal, but is especially effective for those who lead a moderate, healthy and Yogic lifestyle.

Techniques of meditation: Swami Vishnu-devananda has outlined 12 points of meditation in his book *Meditation and Mantras*. This is a summary of his technique taken from *The Sivananda Companion to Yoga*, with additional commentary:

1. Set aside a special place for meditation—the atmosphere you build up will help still the mind. The room needs to be airy, light, clean and pure with an altar as the point of focus.

2. Choose a time when your mind is free of everyday concerns—dawn and dusk are ideal.

3. Using the same time and place each day conditions the mind to slow down more quickly.

4. Sit with your back, neck and head in a straight line, facing north or east. Assume a comfortable cross-legged posture, hands on the knees in chin mudra with the index finger and thumb touching, or with the right hand palm facing upwards on the left palm in the lap. Sit on a blanket or a meditation cushion to alleviate tension in the hips or pressure on the ankles.

5. Instruct your mind to remain quiet for the duration of your meditation session. Turn the mind within and let go of all thoughts through autosuggestion. Repeat Om three times, or chant prayers to get your mind ready.

6. Regulate your breathing—start with five minutes' deep breathing, then slow it down.

7. Establish a rhythmic breathing pattern—inhaling then exhaling for about three seconds. The breath needs to be rhythmic, silent and imperceptible, comfortable yet almost non-existent. Slowly let the breath reduce itself down to an imperceptible rhythm. When the breath becomes calm, the mind automatically becomes calm.

8. At first let your mind wander—it will only grow more restless if you force it to concentrate. After a while, if the mind gets distracted, you can gently bring it back to your point of focus or to your mantra. Be gentle and relaxed. Do not fight with your mind. Repetition of a mantra will create new grooves and uplift your mind from the usual patterns of thought.

9. Now bring the mind to rest on the focal point of your choice—either the Ajna or the Anahata chakra. Once chosen, always keep the same point of focus in order to channel the flow of energy in the same pattern. This is an inner focus on a certain energy center, and it is not a visual looking that involves the eyes. The eyes are kept closed and relaxed.

10. Applying your chosen technique, hold your object of concentration at this focal point throughout your session. The mind cannot focus without an object. In meditation, we need to increase the vibratory level of the mind by focusing the mind on an inspiring object which one holds dear in one's heart. This conscious exercise of concentration will help to counteract the natural distractions of the mind while giving you what you want. It is true that what you think is what you become; therefore, choose a pure object of focus. The most inspiring thought that would lead you to self-realization is the pure vibration of the name of the divine, a sacred mantra. If you do not have a personal mantra (if you have not been initiated into a mantra) then use the universal mantra Om, which you can repeat mentally along with your breath while concentrating your energy at your chosen point of focus. Om is the sound of unity, the basic vibration of the universe, the sound of your breath itself. Focusing on Om in silence will lead you to a place of contentment and harmony deep within you.

11. Meditation comes when you reach a state of pure thought, but still retain your awareness of duality.

12. After long practice, duality disappears and Samadhi, the superconscious state, is attained.

Meditate for half an hour daily. Start with 20 minutes then increase to half an hour, once or twice daily.

* Among the benefits of meditation are: inner strength, peace of mind, a balanced state of mind, concentration, connection with Self, clarity of purpose, and Self-realization. You must experience meditation for yourself. Like sleeping, you cannot really teach someone how to sleep, but you can help someone gather the conditions for meditation to happen.
* The main practice is to meditate daily without expectation.
* The practice of yoga asanas leads to the practice of meditation. They are one and the same.

WHY DO WE CHANT KIRTAN?

Chanting kirtan is a devotional practice that helps to uplift the mind, open the heart and bring inner peace. It is the fastest, easiest and most joyful way to achieve peace of mind. The mantras are mystical universal sounds that resonate with our chakras and remove negative energies. So, it is important that we chant so that we can benefit from this powerful healing energy. It is not about our ego or our self, but it is about chanting the name and the glories of God. We need to chant to express our devotion to something higher than ourselves to open our heart. We need to open our heart daily to the Supreme so that we can live in peace and compassion with all. These kirtans are very old chants composed of mantras which have been given to us by sages and saints. They are in the Sanskrit language which is the language of the Gods, a universal language with pure vibrations corresponding to the vibrations of our chakras, our vital, subtle energy centers. See the chapter on Bhakti Yoga, Gods and Goddesses to get a more detailed explanation of this method of devotional Yoga.

The Sivananda method of chanting:
The Sivananda Organization uses the method of call and response, where the leader of the kirtan chants first and the rest of the group follows out loud. The musical instruments generally used are the harmonium, tablas, tambourines, and other percussion.

To learn to chant, you need only close your eyes, and practice following the sounds, without worrying about how you sound. Beginners can follow along in the Kirtan book, but the book needs to be held so that you can sit erect and connect to the breath. It may be best for you to buy the Kirtan book and CD so that you can bring it home and listen to it daily. Don't worry that it is in Sanskrit or that it is culturally foreign or that you are not a good singer and you don't have a good voice. Eventually you will pick up the chants, and develop a liking for particular chants that correspond to your own inner vibration. It is a devotional, intuitive approach to meditation and not an intellectual one.

The Daily Chants are explained in the chapter on Kirtan. These chants invoke the main aspects of divinity which are in the universe and within us. Though they are Hindu gods, they are not only for Hindus, but represent the subliminal spiritual archetypes within our minds and personalities. Every one of us resonates on a subtle level with a certain vibration and everyone in reality is divine, but we forget ourselves, and chanting the names of God links us with our true divine nature. The different gods represent the different manifestations of the same Supreme Reality. Our expressions in daily life—and even more, our expressions in spiritual life—differ from each other and are unique. This is why it is said, "the paths are many, but the Truth is one". The names or forms are many but God is one.

The Yogic approach to spirituality is very tolerant of cultural differences and respectful of traditions. We understand that you might come from a different spiritual background, but please try to take this as an opportunity for you to understand the concept of Unity in Diversity, and open yourself to other ways of finding union with God, whether you call it Buddha, Jesus, Allah, Mohammed, Guru, Divine Mother, etc. This is what Yoga means by Union—Union with all that seems to be different than ourselves. In that union only, we find peace and health.

We are not trying to convert you to Hinduism or to any other religion. So always try to understand the spirit and the reasons for a certain practice and keep your mind open, without jumping quickly to conclusions. Please be patient with us as it will take time for us to be able to explain all the practices to you. Swami Sivananda says that Yoga is not separate from life but is the spiritualization of all aspects of life.

LABYRINTH AT THE SIVANANDA ASHRAM YOGA FARM

CHAPTER 3

What is Classical Yoga? The Four Paths of Yoga

"Yoga leads us from ignorance to wisdom, from weakness to strength,

from disharmony to harmony, from hatred to love,

from want to fullness, from limitation to infinity,

from diversity to unity, from imperfection to perfection."

– Swami Sivananda in *Bliss Divine*

WHAT IS YOGA?

Yoga is a complete science of life that originated in India many thousands of years ago. It is the oldest system of personal development in the world, encompassing in its scope, body, mind and spirit. The ancient yogis had a profound understanding of man's essential nature and of what he needs to live in harmony with himself and his environment. They perceived the physical body as a vehicle, with the mind as the driver, the soul as man's true identity, and action, emotion and intelligence as the three forces which pull the body-vehicle. In order to have an integral development, these three forces must be in balance. The underlying purpose of all the different aspects of the practice is to reunite the individual Self (the jiva) with the Absolute or pure consciousness (Brahman). The word Yoga means literally "joining". Union with this unchanging reality liberates the spirit from all sense of separation, freeing it from the illusion of time, space and causation. It is only our ignorance, our inability to discriminate between the real and the unreal, that prevents us from realizing our true nature.

Sivananda Yoga teaches the classical method of the four paths of Yoga in order for the individual to experience this state of peace and harmony in the body, mind and spirit. The modern Yoga approach emphasizes the physical postures while classical Yoga includes mental and spiritual components in the practice.

Why do we practice Yoga? We practice Yoga in order to evolve in life, to get success in life and Self-realization. Yoga is not separate from life. It is possible to integrate the practices in our daily routine, no matter our conditions in life (rich or poor, single or with family duties, old or young, healthy or ill), because everyone has spiritual potential and everyone wants to evolve. We are looking for the ultimate answers to all the questions of life: "What is life? What is death? What happens after death? Why do certain people seem to be happier then others? Why are certain people luckier than others? How do we prioritize our life? What is Dharma? What is right? What is wrong? Why is there war and conflict? How can we have peace?"

Yoga practiced as a Sadhana (spiritual practice) gives multiple benefits, physically, mentally and spiritually. Yoga regards the individual in its totality, as a whole, not just as a physical body, or just as an ungrounded mind, or just as a disembodied spirit. Peace and health happen when the individual is in harmony with him or herself, when he is able to perceive himself as one with all, and consequently his actions and feelings are governed by this realization. Yoga brings about physical, mental, emotional and spiritual health.

WHAT IS CLASSICAL YOGA? Classical Yoga is a system of spiritual Knowledge coming from the scriptures (the Vedas), and handed down by a lineage of teachers. It does not come from the creativity of one individual. It is universal and non-sectarian and can be practiced by all. It is a complete system in itself, with many different facets; it is a systematic approach, practiced over a long time, and not a quick fix. The goal is Peace and Self-realization. Its teaching needs to be selfless, to insure the purity of the teaching.

Summary of what Yoga is according to Sivananda's "Bliss Divine"

- Yoga is taking care of body/mind/spirit, not seeking after fitness or beauty, or health.
- Yoga is finding the cause of our suffering; it shows the way to be free from it.
- Yoga is a system of education for the body, the mind, the intellect, and the inner spirit.
- Yoga is a way of life.
- Yoga is universal, not sectarian or separate.
- Yoga helps us to go to the root of our suffering—spiritual ignorance (not knowing who we really are).
- Yoga brings individual peace of mind and collective peace.
- Yoga is unity in diversity.
- Yoga is self discipline.
- Yoga is life.
- Yoga is simple life.
- Yoga is moderate life.
- Yoga helps us to deal with stress.
- Yoga helps calm emotions.
- Yoga is a balanced mind, strong and steady.

THE FOUR PATHS OF YOGA

Swami Sivananda teaches the synthesis of Yoga. He promotes divine life by combining the practice of Karma Yoga (selfless service), Bhakti Yoga (devotional love to God), Hatha Yoga and Raja Yoga (systematic control of body, breath, and mind, culminating in meditation), and, last but not least, Jnana Yoga (or Vedanta philosophy), which is the philosophical teachings of the True Nature of the Self and of the Universe.

His teaching is summarized in his most well known slogan: "Serve, Love, Give, Purify, Meditate, Realize." The tenets and practices of these four paths of Yoga are further explained in subsequent chapters of this book. It is important to remember however, that all the paths lead ultimately to the same destination—to union with Brahman or God—and the lessons of each need to be integrated if true wisdom is to be attained.

Karma Yoga—the Yoga of action—is the path chosen primarily by those of an outgoing nature. It purifies the heart by teaching you to act selflessly, without thought of gain or reward. By detaching yourself from the fruits of your actions and offering them up to God, you learn to sublimate the ego. (See Chapter 11)

Bhakti Yoga is the path of devotion, which appeals particularly to those of an emotional nature. Bhakti Yogis are motivated chiefly by the power of love and see God as the embodiment of Love. Through prayer, worship and ritual, they surrender themselves to God, channeling and transmuting their emotions into unconditional love or devotion. Chanting or singing the praises of God form a substantial part of Bhakti Yoga. (See Chapter 13)

Raja Yoga and Hatha Yoga are the sciences of physical and mental control. They offer a comprehensive method for controlling the waves of thought by turning our mental and physical energy into spiritual energy. (See Chapters 7–10)

Jnana Yoga—the Yoga of knowledge and wisdom—is the most difficult path, requiring tremendous strength of will and intellect. Taking the philosophy of Vedanta, the Jnana Yogi uses his intellect to enquire into his own nature, dissolving the veils of ignorance and illusion. Before practicing Jnana Yoga, the aspirant needs to have integrated the lessons of the other yogic paths—for without selflessness and love of God, and strength of body and mind, the search for Self-realization can become mere speculation. (See Chapter 12)

Even though the practices of the four paths seem to be different in the beginning, they are one and the same and seem different only because of our individual conditioning. In the same manner, we may climb the mountain from different routes, one person preferring to go rock climbing, the other preferring to take it easy on a long winding road, and another preferring the middle path...but at the end all paths lead to the same mountain top. When we reach the top, all paths merge into one. All differences merge into the same essence. Swami Sivananda promotes the integral approach of practicing a little of each path together in daily life, thus exercising our body, head, heart and hands together, integrally, and developing ourselves in all aspects.

Swami Sivananda asserts that we cannot practice any single path of Yoga in isolation. The truth revealed here is that each branch of Yoga involves all the others. For example, there is no Karma Yoga without the right attitude which comes from Bhakti. With the right attitude, whatever work we do can be transmuted into Karma Yoga. We must integrate all the paths of Yoga, pulling the best from each and integrating them into a personal practice.

CHAPTER 4

The Yogic Life: The Five Points of Yoga

"Yoga is a life of self discipline built upon the tenets of simple living and high thinking. If you follow these five points, which compose a true holistic approach to our whole system of body, mind and soul, you will gain strength and balance in this demanding stressful world. Obstacles become stepping stones to success, and life is a school for the development of character and compassion and the Realization of the Divine all-pervading-Self"

- Swami Vishnu-devananda in *The Complete Illustrated Book of Yoga*

BY CLOSELY OBSERVING THE LIFESTYLES and needs of people in our modern world, Swami Vishnu-devananda synthesized the ancient wisdom of Yoga into five basic principles which can easily be incorporated into your own pattern of living, to provide a long, healthy and happy life. The five points of Yoga are:

1. Proper Exercise - Asanas
2. Proper Breathing - Pranayama
3. Proper Relaxation - Savasana
4. Proper Diet - Vegetarian
5. Positive Thinking and Meditation - Vedanta and Dhyana

The body is a vehicle for the soul, and has specific requirements which must be fulfilled for it to function smoothly and supply the optimum mileage. The body can be compared to a car, metaphorically. In order for the car to perform its function, it requires five things: a lubrication system, a battery, a cooling system, proper fuel, and a clear mind and responsible driver behind the wheel.

. PROPER EXERCISE

Proper exercise acts as a lubricating mechanism for the joints, muscles, ligaments, tendons, and other parts of the body, by increasing circulation and flexibility. The fundamental difference between Yogic exercises and ordinary physical exercises is that physical exercises emphasize violent movements of the muscles, while Yogic exercises promote slow and conscious movements of the body, thus avoiding the build-up of lactic acid in the muscle fibers which causes fatigue. The main purpose of exercise is to increase circulation and the intake of oxygen. This can be achieved by simple movements of the spine and various joints of the body, with deep breathing, and without violent movement of the muscles.

Yogic exercises are in fact called yoga asanas, an asana being a steady pose. Yogic exercises, when done correctly, influence and positively energize all systems of the body: the circulatory system, the muscular and skeletal systems, the endocrine system, the respiratory system, the digestive system, and most importantly, the nervous system. In terms of muscles, Yogic exercises not only strengthen the muscles but also stretch them. There is a great emphasis on the flexibility and the youth of the spine. Swami Vishnu-devananda said: "flexible spine, flexible mind."

The correct postures are performed with awareness and concentration, accompanied by breathing and relaxation. Thus Yogic exercises affect not only the physical body but also the astral body, the energetic body and the mind. Through the systematic and rhythmic holding of the postures with breathing and concentration, and releasing the posture to come to a state of relaxation, the prana (or chi) is allowed to flow unobstructed through the nadis to all the organs, cells and parts of the body, revitalizing them. The body and mind are harmonized with each other, removing tension located in the different parts of the body and the mind. Also, in this process, the body and mind are put in alignment or in harmony with their ruler, the Inner spirit, thus giving to the practitioner a deeper sense of well-being and meaning. Yogic asanas prepare the body and mind to be strong for further practice of concentration and meditation.

Other exercises that can be complementary to the practice of Yoga are swimming and walking. Yoga doesn't promote any excessive exercise or the kind of exercise that develops only one aspect of the body to the detriment of other parts. For an exercise to be considered a Yogic exercise, it must be done with awareness. Yogic postures (asanas) are internally-oriented, non-competitive, and meditative, promoting calmness and helping the practitioner to transcend identification with the body, as opposed to our over-attachment to the body and external beauty. (See also Chapter 15)

2. PROPER BREATHING

Yoga emphasizes breathing correctly (the Yogic full breath using the diaphragm). We substantially increase the intake of oxygen through deep inhalation and release the toxins appropriately through our deep exhalation. Yoga teaches us to be constantly aware of our breathing patterns, and to breathe consciously in our daily life. Specific breathing techniques (pranayama) are devised to further purify the nadis, balance the breath and the energy in our system, and to store and channel the subtle energy (prana) for higher purposes.

The word Hatha is composed of the words Ha and Tha, which mean sun and moon, respectively. This refers to the balance between the prana vayu (the positive vital air) and apana vayu (the negative vital air). Prana (vital air) in the body of the individual is a part of the universal breath. The regulation of the harmonized breath helps the Yogi to regulate and steady the mind. Pranayama needs to be practiced by all serious Yoga practitioners. Advanced practices should only be done by those already practicing a pure lifestyle, and it is recommended that they are done under the supervision of a teacher in a pure environment, like an ashram. (See more details on prana in Chapter 8).

3. PROPER RELAXATION

Relaxation techniques, such as Savasana, cool down the system like the radiator of a car. When the body and mind are constantly overworked, their efficiency diminishes. Relaxation is nature's way of recharging the body. The state of our mind and the state of our body are intimately linked. If your muscles are relaxed, then your mind must be relaxed. If the mind is anxious, then the body suffers too. We can say that there are three levels of relaxation: physical, mental and spiritual. There are also three levels of tension, or stress: physical stress, mental stress and spiritual stress.

Physical stress comes from poor eating habits, sedentary living, repetitive movements of the body, and poor posture. Modern life, especially in big cities, is full of stress as modern working and living conditions are full of pressure, and devoid of prana and relaxation. Mental and emotional stress comes from a hectic lifestyle, highly demanding jobs, distractions of the mind, low vitality due to lack of prana, and negative emotions such as anger, hatred, jealousy, fear, and anxiety. Spiritual stress comes from existential anxieties, from living with questions without answers, such as "what is life and death?", "what is love?", "what is the nature of our connections with God?", "is there a God?", "why are there inconsistencies and unrighteousness?", "how can one find stability in the ever-changing phenomena of life?", "why are we suffering from disillusions?", and "why can't we achieve enduring peace?"

The solution is to achieve the three levels of relaxation:
Physical relaxation is achieved through the systematic practice of conscious relaxation (Savasana) and correct posture. Mental relaxation is achieved through correct breathing, concentration of the mind and positive thinking. A distracted mind is always anxious. A mind concentrated on a positive object is more relaxed and recharged. Spiritual relaxation is a deeper type of relaxation, when we become

content, a detached witness of the body and mind. Swami Vishnudevananda states that being free from identification with the body, the mind, and ego-consciousness is the only way to reach a state of complete relaxation. (ref. CIBY, p. 203)

Through complete relaxation we live in the solid present, overcome our fears of death and of the future, and welcome life's demands with strength and courage, able to guide our mind, control our desires and choose better priorities.

4. PROPER DIET

Correct nutrition and diet gives proper fuel for the body and the mind without creating toxins and digestive problems. Optimum utilization of food, air, water and sunlight is essential. There is medical evidence that a balanced vegetarian diet is extremely healthy and provides everything the body needs. The Yogic vegetarian diet is sattvic (pure), and helps to calm the mind, and to reveal the spirit as well as nourish the body.

The body needs food for two purposes: as fuel to supply energy, and as materials to repair body tissues. For repairing and building tissue, the body needs: 1. protein; 2. carbohydrates; 3. fats; 4. minerals. These elements are found in larger proportions in vegetable tissue than in animal tissue. Nuts, peas, beans, soy bean products like tofu, and milk contain protein. Wheat, oats, rice and other grains are mainly carbohydrates. All protein foods and vegetable oils provide the fats, and the main supply of organic minerals and vitamins comes from fruit and vegetables. A vegetarian diet is a natural diet, fresh and wholesome, full of fiber and alkaline in nature, energy-producing, and easy to absorb and to eliminate. To maintain a sattvic diet, free from rajasic and tamasic influences, avoid stimulants and depressants such as caffeine, alcohol, cigarettes, drugs of all kinds, overly spicy food, onions, garlic, overcooked food, old food, frozen food, canned food, sodas and processed foods, as well as all meat. Yogis advocate "ahimsa", the principle of non-violence, non-injury and respect for life. Everything our body and mind needs for growth can be provided from the vegetable kingdom. By avoiding eating animal flesh we nourish ourselves in a natural and healthy way.

The vegetarian diet helps in the performance of asanas as the body and the joints becomes more flexible. It is a wonderful way to prevent heart disease, arthritis, obesity, and a good remedy for many chronic diseases.

Changing to a vegetarian diet can be gradual and life-transforming. It consists not only in deciding to stop eating meat, but in learning a new way of life, by being conscious of how you nourish yourself. It includes not only being aware of what you eat, but also how you eat. Yogis promote taking time to cook, and to eat consciously in a regular manner, with appropriate intervals between meals to allow the digestive fire to activate and digest the food. Blessing meals is also encouraged to sanctify the act of eating and for offering thanks to the Creator. Proper diet includes periodic fasting as well, to give a break to the digestive system, purify body and mind, and to make the mind more perceptive, more sattvic, and more conducive to concentration, contemplation and meditation.

5. POSITIVE THINKING AND MEDITATION

Just as the driver of a car manages to bring himself to his destination without accidents and setbacks, so the yogi learns to manage his mind and emotions in order to keep himself positive at all times. Positive thoughts are energizing and facilitate growth, while negative thoughts are draining and inhibit growth. Only with a positive outlook about oneself can one maintain a meditative life which will ultimately lead to intuitive knowledge and inner strength. (See Chapters 7 and 9.)

CHAPTER 5

Life, Freedom and Happiness

"Happiness comes from within.

It cannot come from without."

– Swami Sivananda in *Bliss Divine*

WHAT IS LIFE?

Yogic concept about life: Swami Sivananda says in *Bliss Divine*, about Life: "Life is God in expression. Life is joy. Life is flooding of the bliss of the Spirit."

Life is like a river. All rivers are restless until they meet the ocean and become one with the ocean. In the same manner, we will be restless until we find the truth about ourselves.

Master also says: "Life is a voyage in the infinite ocean of time, where scenes are perpetually changing. Life is a journey from impurity to purity, from hatred to cosmic love, from death to immortality, from imperfection to perfection, from slavery to freedom, from diversity to unity, from ignorance to eternal wisdom, from pain to eternal bliss, from weakness to infinite strength. Life is a great opportunity provided by the Lord for His children to evolve into Himself."

"The true goal of life is to get back to the source from which we came. The sole object of life is the attainment of Self Realization or absolute freedom. Life in the Spirit is the only real, eternal life. The modern life of rush and hurry, with fear, insecurity, illness and action is not real life. A life of material luxury, of wealth and power, is not the aim of life. Such a life does not produce peace of mind and serenity of soul.

Sensual pleasure is like honey mixed with poison. Sensual enjoyments are attended by various defects, sins, pains, attachments, bad habits, and mental restlessness.

Mundane life is full of sorrows, pain and bondage. It is full of hatred, selfish cares, worries, fights, quarrels, despair and dejections. Any number of zeroes has no value, until you add number 1 before them. Similarly, even if you possess the whole world, it is nothing if you do not lead a spiritual life. Embrace the life of the soul; you will be made pure and free. To live means pursuing the Truth, and surmounting all obstacles with courage. The greatest joy in life is devotion to God, and meditation on God in one's own heart.

To live is to fight for the ideal. Life is a school. The world is your best teacher. There is a lesson in each experience. The world is the best training ground for the development of various divine qualities, such as mercy, forgiveness, tolerance, universal love, generosity, patience, strong will, etc. Give up the lower nature, which consists of selfishness, lust, anger, hatred and jealousy.

Sure way for success in life and God-realization: Make life a perpetual joy. Lead a simple life. Lead a regulated life. Lead a hard life. Live in the present. Forget the past. Give up hopes of the future. Life is thy greatest gift. Utilize every second profitably.

Unity of life: See life as a whole. The Lord breathes in all life. All is one. The world is one home. All are members of one human family. Separation is death. Unity is eternal life. Cultivate cosmic love. Recognize the worth of others. Destroy all barriers that separate man from man. Then this world will be a paradise of beauty, a heaven of peace and tranquility."

Life and the never-ending story of desires: There was a lady living in a thatched hut without electricity. She lost her needle while trying to mend her cloth and went outside of the hut, looking for it desperately. When someone asked her where she lost her needle, she replied, "I lost it in the house".

"So why do you look for it outside?"

She said, "Because inside it is dark, and outside there is light!"

WHAT IS HAPPINESS?

In the same manner, we fail to look within for happiness and continue to search for it in the world of the senses. We become so restless. Why are we restless? It is because we think that there are a lot of things to do, a lot of experiences to have. We have a lot of desires because we think that happiness will come from the satisfaction of desires. But we constantly find ourselves disappointed as the desires, once fulfilled, leave us empty and unfulfilled. Then we wrongly assume that it is the fault of the object and go on changing the object (like changing husbands and yet not finding the perfect one because perfection is within), not realizing that this process is unending and that the true problem lies in our mind which is looking outside for happiness.

Happiness is within, but we look for it in sensual objects. Yoga and meditation help us to calm down, to stop that process of running after desires, and to look within to find the answers.

Relaxation in Yoga is important. Relaxation means ceasing to be restless, and letting go of our attachments and desires. It is also surrendering ourselves or accepting our inner self, and realizing that all is perfect. In the Yoga class, we combine breathing, and relaxation to help people turn inward, relax, slow down, and become aware of themselves.

There is a story of a monkey who put his hand into a jar to get some cookies. He grasped a handful of cookies and tried to pull his hands out of the jar, but his hand was stuck. He became very unhappy and frustrated, jumping around with his hand stuck in the jar, still grasping to the cookies, not realizing that the only way for him to get out of his plight was to drop the cookies. In the same manner, we need to let go of our desires in order for us to enjoy the freedom and happiness that are already here.

WHAT IS FREEDOM?

In Yoga, it is said that freedom can only be attained through self-discipline. True freedom is realizing our inner ruler, the immortal Atman, which is the one without a second. Freedom is the birthright of man. Freedom is the very nature of the Eternal Soul. Freedom is knowledge, peace and bliss. The so-called freedom we enjoy is in fact dependency, resulting from slavery to our desires and the mind. By self-discipline, we control our mind's projections and find true freedom, which is our true nature.

False freedom: Loose life is not perfect freedom. Eating anywhere, sleeping anywhere, aimless wandering, liberty of speech, to be a king, to have plenty, or to possess immense wealth is not freedom. To shirk responsibility is not freedom. Material independence will not give you perfect happiness or freedom.

Real freedom is not merely political or economic. Real Freedom is Lordship over oneself. It is the Freedom of the Soul. It is attainable only through slow and painful stages. Real freedom is freedom from birth and death. Real freedom is freedom from the trammels of flesh and mind. Real freedom is freedom from the bonds of Karma. Real freedom is freedom from desires, wants, likes and dislikes, attachment, lust, anger, greed etc... Real Freedom is identification with the Supreme Self.

The cause of bondage: Mind is the cause of bondage and salvation of man. The egoistic mind is the cause of bondage. Where there is no mind, there is no bondage. Mind imagines, through indiscrimination and ignorance, that the soul has been confined and located in this body, and hence, it perceives the soul to be in bondage. The non egoistic mind is the root of Moksha—or liberation. You have created your own bondage through your desires, attachments, egoism and cravings; you cry for emancipation. Attachment is the most powerful weapon of Maya (cosmic illusion). The first attachment starts with the physical body, and then all other attachments come, attachments to body, food, wife, sons, friend etc... There is no end to cares and worries. Man creates for himself all these cares. No one is to blame.

When there is no I or egoism, there is liberation. It is liberation when the mind is not attached to any object. It is bondage when the mind desires or grieves over anything, rejects or accepts anything, feels angry or happy at anything. Emancipation is release from the bondage of the little ego and its desires and cravings.

Liberation: Know your real divine nature. You are lions, not sheep. This is a story of a baby lion who, growing up amongst sheep, thinks that he is a sheep. He stays baaing like a sheep until a lion comes and brings him to the river to see himself in the reflection of the river. The sheepish lion has mistakes himself to be a sheep, until he sees himself as the same as the lion and realizes his true nature as a lion. He then roars like a lion for the first time, liberating himself from his false concept of himself.

The purpose of Yoga is to free oneself from all false concepts about oneself and realize our immortal Self.

CHAPTER 6

Health, the Three Bodies and the Three Gunas

"Yield not to Tamas and Rajas, stick to Sattva."

– Swami Sivananda

WHAT IS HEALTH? Swami Sivananda says in *Bliss Divine*, "Every human being is the author of his own health or disease. Disease is the result of disobedience to the immutable laws of health that govern life. The laws of health are the laws of nature.

The first wealth is health. It is the greatest of all possessions. It is the basis of all virtues. You should have physical as well as mental health and eventually spiritual health."

THE THREE BODIES

THREE VEHICLES OF THE SOUL

In Yoga we say that we have three bodies: the physical body, the astral body, and the causal body. We need to take care of all three bodies. They are the vehicles of the soul. As in an orange, we have the outer envelope, the peel, then the inside pulp, then the core, or seed. The physical body is like the outer envelope, the astral body is like the pulp, and the causal body is like the seed. The Atman or Self is beyond the three bodies and is said to be the master of the three bodies and independent from them. There are three levels of health, corresponding to the three bodies: physical health, mental health and spiritual health.

1. The physical body:
Physical health is when all the organs function properly under the intelligent control of the mind. A happy person eats well, sleeps well, digests well, and is joyful and productive. The person lives a moderate life according to the law of Nature. The person has self respect and respects Nature.

The physical body is made of the 5 gross elements of nature: earth, water, fire, air and ether. It is said that the physical body corresponds to the food sheath, which is made of food, and will decompose back into the food chain. The Self is not the body; the body is only its vehicle. In the same sense, we might drive a red expensive Mercedes, made in Germany, but it doesn't make us German, nor red, nor worth a few thousands dollars. We constantly make the fundamental mistake of confusing ourselves for our body and superimposing the qualities of our body upon ourselves: male, female, young, old, pretty or ugly, black or white or yellow...The body goes through constant changes, from childhood, to adulthood, to old age, ending in death. Yet the soul is not affected. The Bhagavad Gita says that the soul casts off the body like an old garment and puts on new ones. If you look at various photos of yourself taken during different phases of your physical development, from the body of a baby, to a child, to an adolescent, and an adult, you can see the proof. Looking at these different bodies and different features, you still claim that "this is me", "this is me"....and yet this "me" has nothing to do with the completely different bodies. To add to the argument, all the cells of the body change every seven years and yet we maintain a basic identity within these changes. Detachment from the body is the basis of all health.

2. The astral body:
The astral body, also called subtle body, is composed of the energy sheath (pranic sheath), the mind, the emotions, the intellect and the ego. A sheath is like an envelope or a veil which obscures the vision of the Self. Yogic practices help to remove the veil or see through the veil, and bring clarity of vision.

The pranic sheath is like our etheric envelope, our aura, radiating from our physical body, made up of our prana. Thus you can literally feel the

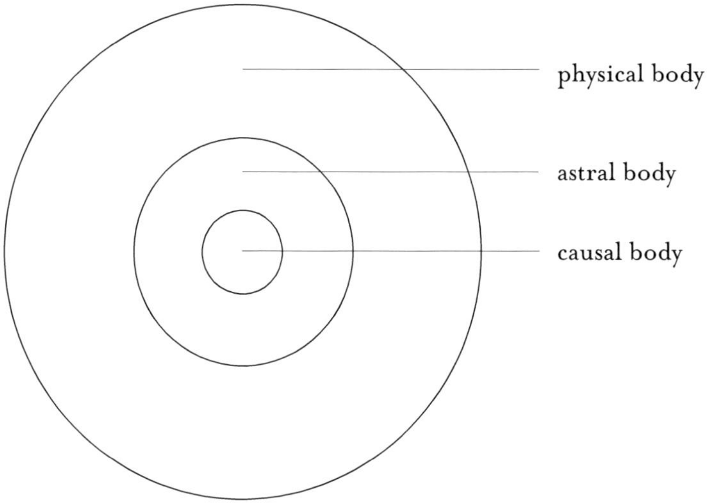

presence of someone in a room, or his or her absence, from the quality of the prana we feel in the room. We can photograph the etheric body with Kirlian photography, for example, and see the state of health of our pranic sheath. The pranic sheath is transcended through pranayama and proper diet.

The mental sheath is the subtle layer of our mind, emotions and senses. It is the storehouse of all our past thoughts and experiences, as well as our instincts and lower emotions. This mind can be negative or positive. If negative, it is contracted, and manifests as a blockage of energy. If positive, it is expanded and is full of prana and light. The mental sheath can be transcended through positive thinking, concentration and meditation. We achieve mental health when we are focused, balanced, calm and positive, and when the mind is free from desire, addiction, and is sattvic.

The intellectual sheath is our faculty of reasoning, discriminating and making decisions. The intellect can be used positively, or negatively to serve our lower mind and desires. It can be transcended through self-inquiry, discrimination and meditation.

The ego is the false sense of self, the principle of separateness which we need to overcome in order for us to be healthy, mentally and spiritually. The ego can be removed through selfless service, universal love, and self-inquiry.

3. The causal body:

The seed body is a deeper layer of our self in which lays the seed of our ignorance and in which we store our karmic seeds. This means that unless we remove the cause of our ignorance, we will continue to repeat the same mistakes, actions and reactions, lifetime after lifetime. Spiritual health dawns when we understand the cause of our ignorance, which is responsible for our suffering, and learn to be detached from our karmic patterns. We become aware of the consciousness which underlies all phenomena and circumstances. It is said that the causal body is also known as the bliss sheath, because of its proximity to the Atman or Soul.

THE THREE GUNAS

UNDERSTANDING THE QUALITIES
LEADING TO HEALTH AND DISEASE

There are three qualities in nature, called Gunas:

1. **Tamas** is the quality of inertia, darkness and ignorance. If the mind is tamasic the person will be lazy, depressed, and negative. Tamasic food and tamasic lifestyle lead to diseases and blockages in the flow of prana.

2. **Rajas** is the quality of activity, passion, action, egoism, and indulgence. If the mind is rajasic, the person will be passionate, competitive, busy with self-centered activities, and full of desires. Among other causes, excess Rajas causes stress. Rajasic food and rajasic lifestyle can also bring disharmony and diseases that come from the disturbances of the flow of prana.

3. **Sattva** is a quality of purity, balance, knowledge, wisdom and discipline. The sattvic mind is clear, focused, harmonious and connected (with self and others). Sattvic food, sattvic company, and sattvic environments bring about health.

A healthy body, mind and spirit are sattvic. Yoga life brings Sattva to body, mind and spirit. Yoga practice brings clarity, concentration, connectedness, calmness, harmony, and intuition, and, ultimately, health.

Practicing the five points of Yoga will increase Sattva, remove Tamas, and calm down Rajas so our life will not alternate up and down. Tamas is like a thick veil over our consciousness. Rajas is like a constant projection of ideas that create fragmentation, division, separation, and conflict. Sattva is like a clear lake in which you can see a true reflection of yourself.

REFLECTIONS

CHAPTER 7

Mind, Its Mysteries and Control

"Conquest of mind is very hard indeed; but not impossible. Therefore try and try, again and again, you will succeed at last."

—Swami Sivananda in *Elixir Divine*

THE MIND IS IN THE ASTRAL BODY, and is subtle and powerful. It is our instrument of perception. Like a pair of glasses which you use to see through, the defects or tint of the glasses will make you perceive defects outside and will color what you see. In *Bliss Divine* Swami Sivananda says about the mind, "The activity of the mind is the cause of all appearances. So long as there is the mind, there are all these distinctions of big and small, high and low, inferior and superior, good and bad, etc... But the thinker is different from thought. Mind is as much your property and outside of you as your limbs, the dress you wear and the building you dwell in."

WHY DO WE NEED TO CONTROL THE MIND?

What we perceive externally is in fact a reflection of the quality and conditioning of our mind. If we are angry then we will find a reason to be angry about anything. If we are depressed, everything looks depressing, and so on. The whole world is in our mind. We have the feeling that the world is a big place and we have no control over it. We feel victimized by a lot of things. Yoga helps us to regain clarity and power by helping us to control our mind. The process of going inward to find answers means finding out the conditioning of our mindset and adjusting it to reality, thus bringing us to a true vision of ourselves and of reality, and freeing us from seeing distortions or illusions.

To be able to control the mind, we have to be detached from it and know that the mind is not us, but only our instrument. In the same manner, a cloud covering the sun may make us think that the sun is not there, but if we know that the sun is always there, then we can feel and see that the black and cold is just a temporary state. The mind can go through different states but you can make it change if you don't believe in what you see or feel as being yourself. You stay detached, and you know that the mind is not you. Instead of saying, "I am angry", you say, "There is anger in my mind." Instead of saying, "I hate this person", you say, "There is hatred in my mind." Yoga, by slowing down the body and mind, helps you cultivate this process of detachment.

Now, we will give you a few analogies in order to help you to understand the mechanics of the mind and to recognize your own mind. Because we are not aware of the functioning of the mind, we become victim to it. Learning how the mind functions is like learning how to drive a car, so that we are able to guide the mind instead of the mind creating havoc without our control.

1. Mind is like a lake; it constantly has thought waves. Swami Sivananda says that the mind "havocs" through the power of fluctuation. That is why the meditator endeavors to calm the thought waves down by concentration. A clear lake without waves is capable of giving you a true reflection of yourself (sattvic mind); a wavy lake distorts the reflection (rajasic mind); a muddy lake will not allow you to see clearly (tamasic mind).

2. Mind is like a drunken monkey; it is very restless and jumpy. Swami Sivananda says that the mind has wandering habits. It wants variety. Thoughts are disorderly and random, without much continuity or focus. Know this and learn to keep the mind more focused.

3. Mind is like a wild horse; it does not like to be tamed but likes to go its own way. Like a spoiled kid or a badly trained animal, the mind does not like to be trained and follows its own will, resisting all

attempts to control it. Thus, one has to be gentle with the mind and slowly gain its trust to guide it in the right direction.

4. Mind is like a shy lady; it likes to hide and not be seen. It is difficult to reveal the secrets of the mind, as it will not cooperate easily. However, when one is able to see it for what it is, the turbulent mind calms itself down.

5. Mind is like a music record; it has grooves and habits. Everyone's mind is conditioned specifically by previous experiences and habits. Sometimes, the record is scratched and bad tunes are played - as in the case of our repeated bad patterns—we need help sometimes to lift the needle and change the groove to a more positive habit.

6. Mind is like a fast-spinning fan; it can move very fast and you cannot distinguish the thoughts, but the thoughts can harm you. This is why, in Yoga, we learn to slow down the thought waves through asanas, pranayama and self observation in order to switch the patterns of thought. This analogy also shows that the concentrated mind is very powerful; a concentrated person may appear to be doing nothing, and yet his mind is extremely active.

7. Mind is related to body; that is why if you straighten your posture (asana), you straighten your mind. Asana practice is the best way to begin controlling the mind.

8. Mind is related to the breath; that is why if you calm down your breath and control the prana (pranayama), you control the mind. The breath is like the wind that creates the waves on the lake; it is difficult to control the waves, but if there is no wind, there are no waves.

9. Mind is related to the senses; controlling the senses will calm down the mind and controlling the mind can reduce the effect of the sensory stimulation that would agitate the mind. If the mind is kept focused, the senses will not operate, as the senses cannot operate without the cooperation of the mind. The idea is that we are not victims to sensual influences and that we have ways to escape the allurements of the senses.

10. Mind, although fast, can only think of one thought at a time; if you feel stressed out, simply do one thing at a time. This is an important idea as it helps us to understand what concentration is, and why we need to concentrate on a positive thought, like a mantra, in order to reduce stress and worry.

11. Mind functions with names and forms; the mind itself is limited as it only functions along with words and images. This is why we use words or images to focus on; we understand that words and images are the limited way to express the reality that is beyond the grasp of the mind. This world as we know it is just the world of names and forms, and there is another reality beyond it. That reality can be experienced only when we go beyond the mind.

12. The mind functions by association. We can use this associative tendency of the mind to eliminate unhelpful thoughts and accentuate helpful thoughts.

Yoga is the science of mind. It includes working with the three levels of our mind: the subconscious, the conscious and the super-conscious. Yogis want to clear the subconscious (instincts and emotions), fully utilize the conscious (intellect) and develop the super-conscious (intuition). This can be achieved through Yoga and meditation practice.

ANULOMA VILOMA (PRANAYAMA)

CHAPTER 8

Prana and Kundalini

"The Yogi, using the method of pranayama, is able to absorb the energy from the infinite mass that exists behind, uses this energy for his quick spiritual growth, and within a short time is able to reach the highest perfection."

- Swami Vishnu-devananda in *The Complete Illustrated Book of Yoga*

WHAT IS PRANA?

Prana is vital energy that is everywhere in the universe. It is all pervading. Prana is the link between the astral and the physical bodies. Death takes place when the prana that is working in the physical body is withdrawn in the astral body. Breath is the external manifestation of prana, the vital force. Breath is gross. Prana is subtle. By exercising control over the gross breath, you can control the subtle Prana inside. The aim of pranayama is the control of prana. If you can control prana, you can completely control all the forces of the universe, mental and physical.

If prana is everywhere, why do we sometimes feel that we don't have enough prana? The reason is that we don't know how to recharge ourselves, and we do more to spend prana than we do to re-supply. If you have prana debts, you start to have disease. It starts with stress, and it ends up in physical disease. Recent scientific research indicates a strong correlation between mental, emotional stress, and the onset of physical disease, including cancer.

HOW CAN YOU RECHARGE YOUR PRANA?

There are five ways to supply prana to the system:

1. Through the earth element: natural food, living in nature, walking on the ground, contemplating trees, walking barefoot. People living in big cities may lose prana from working and sleeping in concrete buildings, walking on pavement, traveling by car or by subway, not having many trees around, and eating fast food in a hurry...

2. Through the water element: drink spring water, swim in a river, or the ocean. Avoid drinking soda, alcohol, or caffeinated drinks because these drain more prana than they supply.

3. Through the fire element: Prana is supplied by being in the sun and eating food that contains sunlight.

4. Through the air element: This is the most important way to get prana, through breathing fresh air. Avoid polluted and crowded places, smoking cigarettes etc...

5. Through the ether element: Prana is supplied through being in a positive thought atmosphere because thought is transmitted through ether. In crowded places like cities, subways, hospitals, you absorb lots of negative thoughts that drain your prana. On the contrary, if you are in ashrams, monasteries, temples, churches, you automatically feel good because the thought atmosphere is positive and calm.

WHAT DO WE NEED TO DO WITH PRANA?

We need an abundant supply of prana to be healthy and to provide energy for our daily activities, but as yogis, we need prana for our spiritual path.

Yogis are endeavoring to:

1. Increase prana and store it for spiritual evolution (by the practice of pranayama and by the yogic lifestyle)
2. Conserve prana (learn how not to waste it through worries, useless thinking and conversation, purposeless activities, too much indulgence in sensual pleasures)
3. Balance prana (learn to balance our energy and personality and avoid extremes)
4. Channel prana (use it for positive goals, through selfless action, chanting, etc.)
5. Purify prana (through pranayama and through our choice of company and activities, the yogi endeavors to elevate the vibration of his thought)

THE ASTRAL BODY

We have 72,000 nadis, or meridians, which circulate prana throughout the body. Practicing asanas helps distribute the prana, and free energy blockages; pranayama helps to balance prana, and also to increase our supply.

Positive thinking helps to increase positive thoughts in the mind, and thus creates positive prana in the system.

Meditation helps us connect with the unlimited supply of prana in the universe.

Chakras, Kundalini and Spiritual Evolution

There are seven chakras in the astral body: Muladhara chakra, Swadhisthana chakra, Manipura chakra, Anahata chakra, Vishudha chakra, Ajna chakra and Sahasrara chakra. These energy centers represent the stages of consciousness and are located along the Sushumna nadi, which is the central channel corresponding to our spinal column. The Ida and Pingala are the nadis through which the prana flows prior to entering the Sushumna. When the prana flows through the Ida and Pingala, the individual experiences duality (i.e. hot and cold, pleasure and pain, up and down, etc.). This means our experience is of incompleteness and separation and the suffering which comes with them. There are many popular ideas about purification and manipulation of the chakras that do not correspond to the classical theory. The chakras represent stages of consciousness and opening of the chakras requires complete transformation of consciousness and not mere manipulation of external energy.

The Sushumna Nadi is open and activated only when purification takes place. At that time, it is said that the Kundalini Shakti is awakened.

PURIFICATION FOR KUNDALINI AWAKENING

Purification happens only when the individual is selfless, pure, sattvic, balanced and aspires to God-realization. The nadis get impure when the ego is operating, creating desires. Purification happens through Karma Yoga, service to Guru, Bhakti Yoga, methods of Hatha Yoga like pranayama and kriyas, meditation, positive thinking and self-inquiry.

It cannot happen by force or through technique alone, or because of personal ambition or desire. So, the Yoga practitioner needs to be patient and improve him or herself without expectation. There is a lot of misunderstanding about Kundalini; most people just want short-cuts and are only impressed by external demonstrations of supernatural powers. Our emotional mind likes to dream but not to take up the discipline to change ourselves.

Kundalini is the cosmic energy lying dormant at the base of the spine in the Muladhara Chakra. It is a cosmic spiritual potential present in everybody in a dormant state. Kundalini awakening requires strong discipline and purification in all aspects. Swami Vishnu-devananda said that wherever there is supernatural power, wisdom or knowledge, there must be at least a partial manifestation of Kundalini.

In conclusion, we must know that theoretical knowledge of the various pranas, pranayamas and chakras is helpful for Hatha yogis to know the path, but that the nature of the spiritual path is not merely technical. Swami Sivananda prescribed the synthesis of Yoga for a complete purification of all aspects of life. When purification takes place, the Kundalini will be automatically awakened. Hatha Yoga, Kundalini Yoga, Mantra Yoga, and Raja Yoga are one and the same, even though the emphasis is slightly different in each. They are all part of Ashtanga Yoga (the yoga of eight limbs—see Chapter 10).

SWAMI VISHNU-DEVANANDA

CHAPTER 9

Thought Power and Positive Thinking

"There is a power contained in thought. This is very subtle, yet it does exist, and is extremely powerful. Whether a person is aware of it or not, he is constantly transmitting and receiving thoughts... Thoughts control our lives, mold our characters, shape destiny, and affect other people. When the potential contained in the power of thought is realized, it is the beginning of great spiritual growth in the individual; a great step forward for all of humanity."

- Swami Vishnu-devananda in *Meditation and Mantras*

WHAT IS THOUGHT?

Thought is a powerful force or energy which can build and can destroy. It is real. We need to be aware of the nature of our thoughts in order to improve our life and to keep meditating and ultimately realizing our perfect positive nature. Negative thoughts are like toxins produced by the mind that is not purified. They are only temporary symptoms, not ourselves.

Thought, though invisible, is the origin of action and the material world. We make a mistake when we think that the material world of objects is more real than the world of thought. Objects are manifestations of thoughts—the Sivananda ashram for example, came from the thoughts of Swami Vishnu-devananda.

Thought has different wavelengths. Positive thoughts or Sattvic thoughts have higher wavelength and negative thoughts have lower wavelength. We are constantly swimming in an ocean of thoughts, attracting certain thoughts and repulsing others, depending on the quality of the thoughts we keep in our mind. The best way to improve our life is to constantly keep positive thoughts in our mind and to be able to change negative thoughts to positive thoughts.

Be aware of thought influences. We need to be aware of the thought that is surrounding us, it affects our thinking. Try to keep positive company, live and work in positive environments, be in nature, and take Yoga retreats to retune the mind to positive thoughts. Also, learn internal techniques to keep the mind at a high wavelength, so instead of being victims of our environment, we will be agents of positive change. Being in company of the wise is the easiest and most powerful way to shift our thinking to be more positive. This is called Satsanga, company of the wise. When you live in an ashram founded by enlightened masters, you are in Satsanga. The vibrations of all the chanting, teachings and all the good thoughts of people who visited or lived in the ashram remain in the thought atmosphere and help you. It is like taking a bath in a pool of pure water. If you mix with polluted thought environments, you will pick up negative thoughts that you would not normally have.

Thought creates destiny. Thought has the tendency to repeat itself; a negative thought or feeling can become habitual, and also a positive thought can create a positive personality or character that will bring about your future destiny. So destiny is in your hands, if you know how to control your thoughts.

One needs to be responsible for one's thoughts because one's thoughts affect the invisible thought world, and in turn, affect the environment and the people around you positively or negatively. Collective negative thinking can create wars, while collective positive thinking, like our group here sitting in the ashram, chanting and meditating, sends positive vibrations out to the whole world.

Thought is immediate. So, its effect is immediate, transcending time and space. It is much faster than any supercomputer or the Internet. Only now, scientists and philosophers are starting to discover the power of thoughts—for example, the Japanese scientist Doctor Emoto has demonstrated the power of thought and emotions on water. Since our body is made up of seventy to ninety percent water, you can imagine the effect a negative thought environment can have on us.

POSITIVE THINKING TECHNIQUES

1. First, be aware of the nature of the negative thought. Learn to recognize the nature of your thought and evaluate its importance by seeing how frequently it occurs in your mind. Study the different thoughts—for example, knowing that unfulfilled desires are the root cause of anger will help you remove that anger by letting go of the corresponding desires. Fears come from attachment and so on.

2. Have the conviction that it is not worth keeping the negative thought in the mind for any length of time because it will get more serious, like a cold that could develop into the flu or pneumonia, if you don't take care of it.

3. Try different methods to change the thought (see the Thought Tool Box, next page). Know that you are your own doctor, and you can help yourself by changing your thoughts. Know also that you have choices; one method might not work, but others will and your favorite way might not be the appropriate one. Ultimately, thought is not you, and it is changeable. Allow yourself to be flexible and not stuck in one way of thinking or reacting.

4. Classical Yoga methods— the four paths (Chapter 3) and the five points (Chapter 4)—train you to prevent negative thoughts; a sattvic mind is automatically positive. You can develop positive attitudes toward negative events, and thus transform your frame of mind.

THOUGHT TOOL BOX

Everyone has the power to transform their thought from being negative to being positive. As thought is immediate, one needs to master these different tools at our disposal in order to replace a negative thought with an appropriate positive thought. It is good to do it immediately and not wait too long as the negative thought becomes more serious over time, by the power of repetition.

The classical Yoga paths offer some techniques for positive thinking:

a. Following the Bhakti Yoga school of thought, a devotee practices faith and self surrender to God's will. He believes that "everything happens all the time for the best", and says to himself, "It's not my will, it's God's will, and I surrender to God's will". He practices chanting and repeats mantras with devotion as well as endeavors to see God in all beings and in Nature.

b. From Raja Yoga we learn a few techniques to directly deal with our mind:
   - replacing negative thoughts with opposite thoughts
   - being indifferent to negative thoughts
   - sublimating, channeling, or transforming negative thoughts into less harmful thoughts
   - focusing the mind on the positive only
   - practicing visualization of yourself endowed with the positive qualities you seek
   - repeatedly self-affirming with helpful words
   - maintaining a cheerful attitude
   - being careful of impatience when trying to change, one thought at a time
   - staying vigilant to the fact that a negative thought will bring in its associates, and that a positive thought will bring in a train of thoughts which will uplift you
   - being in Satsanga or positive company

c. From the Karma Yoga perspective, the Karma Yogi constantly reminds himself, amidst action, that, "I am not the doer, I am only an instrument. I offer the results of my work," and, "I do the best I can, and I do my duty."

d. From the Jnana Yoga philosophical standpoint, the Jnana Yogi reminds himself, "I am only the silent witness to this; everything is but an illusion; everything is changing anyway, this also shall pass; I am the Self of all, therefore no one can hurt me nor take away anything from me; I am Sat Chit Ananda—pure consciousness, bliss absolute, therefore nothing can touch me. We are one, this person is my own self, the whole world is my own self." By thinking so, the Yogi removes the root cause of all negativities and remains detached.

SIVA HILL AT THE SIVANANDA ASHRAM YOGA FARM

CHAPTER 10

The Eight Limbs of Raja Yoga

"In the beginning of your Sadhana, you will encounter various difficulties. You will not be conscious of any spiritual progress, but you will be conscious of your failures in your attempts in meditation, the resistance you meet, your defects and weaknesses."

–Swami Sivananda in *Sivananda Upanishad*

RAJA YOGA IS THE PATH OF systematic analysis and control of the mind. Compiled by Patanjali Maharishi, Raja Yoga is also known as Ashtanga Yoga, because its practices can be divided into eight limbs. Hatha Yoga, Kundalini Yoga, and Mantra Yoga are all parts of Raja Yoga. The goal is to control the chitta vrittis, or thought waves, and thus attain the super-conscious state of mind, the final goal.

The eight limbs are:

1. **YAMAS** - the restrictions
    a. **Ahimsa:** non-violence, non-injury. Vegetarianism is part of the practice of ahimsa. The great Indian saint Gandhi is famous for the practice of ahimsa.
    b. **Satya:** truthfulness, not telling lies
    c. **Brahmacharya:** chastity, sublimation of sexual energy
    d. **Asteya:** non-stealing, non-covetousness, lack of jealousy
    e. **Aparigraha:** non-accepting of gifts or bribes

2. **NIYAMAS** - the observances
    a. **Saucha:** purity (external and internal)
    b. **Santosha:** contentment
    c. **Tapas:** austerity
    d. **Swadhyaya:** study of religious scripture
    e. **Ishwara Pranidhana:** worship of the Lord, surrender of the ego

3. **ASANA** - steady pose (see Chapter 15). For spiritual pursuit, as for any other pursuit in life, a healthy and strong system is essential. A steady mind presupposes a steady body.

4. **PRANAYAMA** - control of the vital energy.

5. **PRATYAHARA** - withdrawal of the senses from objects.

6. **DHARANA** - concentrating the mind upon either an external object or an internal idea, to the exclusion of all other thoughts.

7. **DHYANA** - meditation is defined as an unbroken flow of thought towards God to the exclusion of other sensual perception.

8. **SAMADHI** - super-conscious state.

Note that the Yamas and Niyamas constitute the ethical foundation of the Yoga practice, straighten out the mind, and help reduce agitations and restlessness. Asana, Pranayama and Pratyahara are external practices, while Dharana, Dhyana and Samadhi are considered advanced internal practices.

Even though there is an idea of progression in the practices, one doesn't have to wait for ethical perfection before attempting concentration and meditation. In fact, all the stages are involved together. For example, one cannot meditate if one doesn't have good posture and possess a certain calmness of breath, thus achieving an inner focus at the exclusion of everything else.

The practice of concentration is the preliminary practice for meditation. Concentration is holding one thought in the mind for a period of time. Concentration brings power to the mind and makes the mind one-pointed, thus allowing peace and happiness to shine through. Concentration implies effort and perseverance to bring the mind back to focus.

Concentration on an external object—like a candle flame (tratak)—is easier than focusing internally on an abstract idea. There are many exercises for concentration; for example, allowing the mind to think of a topic and everything related to the topic but nothing outside of the topic. The mind is like a sheep tied to a post, and has to move in a smaller circle. The fewer thoughts you have in the mind, the more peace you have. The more thoughts in the mind, the less peace you have. Concentration is like gathering the rays of the mind and applying them to a particular topic. In the same manner that gathering the rays of the sun through a magnifying glass can burn a piece of paper, or gathering the water of a stream through a dam can produce electricity, the Yogi endeavors to have fewer thoughts, so the thoughts that remain in the mind will gain power and realization.

A concentrated person is much more productive, effective and peaceful, while a distracted person is unfulfilled, constantly changing topics, and never finishes anything.

Through concentration, the mind moves through stages, and with the stages, develops more peace and happiness. There are five states of concentrative minds:

1. dull state - there is unhappiness and depression
2. scattered state of mind - there is unhappiness and restlessness
3. gathered state of mind - the mind is more calm and productive
4. one-pointed state of mind - the mind is nearly in a meditative state
5. total absorption of the mind - the mind loses itself

The main contribution of Raja Yoga is knowledge of the mind and how to harness the powers of the mind for higher purpose. Yoga Psychology is the knowledge of the mind in order to transcend the mind.

KARMA YOGA IN THE GARDEN

CHAPTER 11

Karma and Karma Yoga

"The first step in the spiritual path is the selfless service to Humanity"

—Swami Sivananda in *Sivananda Upanishad*

WHAT IS KARMA?

Karma literally means "action". Action always comes with the consequence of the action. The law of karma is the law of action and reaction, illustrated by the well-known saying "what we reap is what we sow," and also the law of retribution, which explains that "what we receive is the result of what we did in the past." Nothing is by accident, merit, demerit, honor, or dishonor; any happening in our lives is the result of karma.

The philosophy of karma is the foundation of all oriental philosophical thought, Hindu and Buddhist. Understanding how this law applies in life helps us to spiritualize our lives and progress.

It is said that there are three kinds of karma: past karma, present karma and future karma. The three are interrelated; present karma is the result of past karmas, and is our reaction to the past, and will determine our future karmas. This body and mind are nothing but the result of past karma. These past karmic impressions have the tendency to reproduce themselves and determine our circumstances and choices. Our reactions to what has happened determine if we will learn the spiritual lessons or not. The residue of what needs to be learned will unfold in another context later on.

Karma is neither good nor bad. From the point of view of the Atman, or soul, karma is that which binds us to the wheel of birth and death. The goal of the Yogi is to break through the chain of karma and release himself from all bondage caused by spiritual ignorance. This release from karma is gradual, as many lessons need to be learned and many experiences gathered for the individual to truly understand the Truth, which is the only thing that can set him free.

What is Karma Yoga?

"Karma Yoga is the Selfless Devotion of all the inner and outer activities as a sacrifice to the Lord of All Works, offered to the Eternal as Master of all the Soul's energies and austerities." — BHAGAVAD GITA

"Work done in the right attitude becomes consecrated; becomes a sacred act."
"A life consecrated to doing selfless acts will become a divine life."
— SWAMI SIVANANDA

As our life is the result of karma, our life itself holds the key to our liberation. The idea is to spiritualize our life and our actions in order to be free. The problem is that we are very attached to our actions and our works; we constantly identify with our actions and take pride in what we are doing. Our ego is very much invested in our talents, skills, knowledge and activities. It takes detachment towards our actions in order to see ourselves and our actions in a different light. In the cultivation of the spirit of Karma Yoga lies our freedom and spiritual release.

KARMA YOGA GUIDELINES

1. Right Attitude

It is not what you do that counts, it is the attitude while doing it that determines whether it is a job or Karma Yoga (i.e., a binding or a liberating job). Work is worship. Swami Sivananda advised that you should, "Give your hands to work and keep your mind fixed at the Lotus Feet of the Lord."

2. Right Motive

This is similar to right attitude; it is not what you do that counts but your real motive behind it. Your motive must be pure. Swami Sivananda says, "Man generally plans to get the fruits of his work before he starts any kind of work. The mind is so framed that it cannot think of any kind of work without remuneration or reward. A selfish man cannot do any service. He will weigh the work and the money in a balance. Selfless service is unknown to him."

Consider the example of two girls who were drowning. Two young men immediately jumped in to help them. One man jumped in so he could ask the girl to marry him. The other said only, "I have done my duty. God gave me an opportunity to serve and improve myself." The external action was the same, but the inner motive was different.

3. Do Your Duty (Swadharma)

Often our specific duty in life is referred to as "Swadharma", which means "righteousness". Performance of duty frees the soul, and non-performance of duty keeps the soul in bondage. Perform your duty according to your caste and your stage in life, which are created by the gunas or qualities born from a person's nature. The highest duty is to God, the In-dweller, to learn and to progress.

4. Do your best

Whatever you do, do your best. You will incur demerit if you do not give your best. If you know of a better way to serve then you must make use of it. You cannot hold back from fear of the effort required or from fear of criticism. Do not do work in a sloppy manner because no one is watching or because the work is not for you. Give your best effort. Try to do actions that can bring maximum good and minimum evil. Try at all times to accumulate merits. Do Karma Yoga increasingly often as this will accelerate your paying off of karmic debts. There is no time to lose.

Swami Sivananda has said, "You can elevate others only if you have elevated yourself. A prisoner cannot liberate other prisoners."

5. Give up results

God is the Doer. You are not the Doer; you are only the Instrument. You do not know God's intentions or God's plans. God is the actor (i.e. the Self never acts). It is only the gunas that are playing. The way to realize this Truth is to constantly work for work's sake and to let go of the outcome, good or bad.

It is the desire for action that binds the individual. (I am the doer is wrong knowledge.) It is detachment from action (I am only the instrument is right knowledge) that will dissolve the Karmic seeds.

Detachment from results also means detachment from the type of job itself. There are neither inferior nor superior jobs. Don't be attached to your job and be ready to give up your job when necessary. Note that Karma is always working. You will always be drawn to things that you need to learn.

6. Serving God or the Self in All

Do unto others what you would like to have done to yourself. Love thy neighbor as thyself. Adapt, adjust, accommodate. Bear insult, bear injury. Unity in diversity. We are all parts of the same body. Practice humility in action. Beware of power, fame, name, praise, and censure.

7. Follow the discipline of the job

Every work experience has something to teach you. Try to do your best and the lessons of your work will be rich. Each job involves different requirements in terms of time, degree of concentration, skills or experience, emotional input, physical energy, and will.

8. Qualifications of a Karma Yogi

"A Karma Yogi should be free from lust, greed, anger, and egoism. He should try to remove these. He should be humble and free from hatred, jealousy, harshness, etc. A Karma Yogi should have an amiable, loving, and sociable nature. He should be able to move and mix with everybody without distinction of caste, creed, or color. He should have perfect adaptability, mercy, and cosmic love. He should be sympathetic and tolerant. He should be able to adjust himself to the habits and ways of others. He should always have a cool and balanced mind. He should have equal vision. He should rejoice in the welfare of others. He should lead a very simple life.

A Karma Yogi should have a sound, healthy, and strong physical body. He should do regular pranayama, physical exercise, and asanas in order to keep up a high standard of health. He should have power of endurance."

— SWAMI SIVANANDA

What will the practice of Karma Yoga bring? How will it help you?

- You will develop and learn new skills.
- It will help personality growth, health, and fulfillment.
- It will thin out the ego and remove selfishness.
- You will achieve purification of the heart.
- You will overcome the "likes and dislikes" of your mind.
- You will eliminate prejudices.
- You will feel oneness, unity and unbounded joy.
- You will become more loving, balanced, and sattvic.
- You will have a more flexible mind and a more tolerant attitude (less rigid).
- You will broaden your outlook on life.
- It allows you to spiritualize your activities.
- It will keep you focused on God throughout the day.

SWAMI SIVANANDA

CHAPTER 12

Who Am I? Vedanta Philosophy of the Self and the Not-Self

"Solve first the, "Who am I?" problem.

All other problems will be automatically solved."

—SWAMI SIVANANDA in *Sivananda Upanishad*

WHAT IS VEDANTA PHILOSOPHY?

Yoga philosophy is called Vedanta philosophy—it comes from the scripture called the Vedas. The term Vedanta is derived from the Sanskrit root "Vid" meaning "to know" and "Anta" meaning "end." Thus Vedanta literally means "the end of knowledge." Vedanta philosophy is so-called because it explains what the end is and how to achieve it. It is a philosophy that teaches the unity of life, or oneness of consciousness. It is the sublime philosophy which boldly proclaims that the individual Soul (the jiva) is identical with the Supreme Soul or Brahman. It is the only philosophy that can reunite—on the basis of the one common Self in all—different religions, cultures, races and personalities. This knowledge has been given to us by the Rishis, enlightened sages who attained the highest level of knowledge. The Rishis taught that the nature of the Atma or the Self is Sat Chit Ananda.

THE SELF AS SAT-CHIT-ANANDA

Sat means existence absolute. It means that we are the immortal soul; we have never been born and we never die. We have a body simply to work out karma; it is temporary. Always remember that other dimension of ourselves which is beyond the body and its relationships, and the changes that occur while in the body. (Relationships with family members relate only to the body and karmas of this particular lifetime; we need to fulfill duties, but with the awareness that this learning experience is solely for our personal growth.and not about the countless fathers, mothers, husbands, and wives, and children of this lifetime or past lives. Detachment is also necessary when the body is getting older, diseased, and, eventually, dying). Therefore, always remember the immortal Self and be detached from the body, and unafraid of death.

Chit means knowledge absolute. It means that we are the self of all; we know everything because we are the consciousness of all. We are the witness or observer of all changing phenomena, all changing names and forms. Take the analogy of the screen that remains the same while different movies are playing on it, or of the actor who remains the same despite all the different roles he plays. Knowledge, according to Yoga, is not just intellectual or academic, it is self-knowledge which comes from experience of the Truth. Yoga is a scientific method to find the Truth.

Ananda means bliss absolute. This means that all our suffering is illusory. It is like when a tiger is chasing you in a dream, and you become very scared. The only thing you can do to escape the tiger is to wake up. For a yogi, this world is like a dream, and while it is relatively real, it is only real when you are sleeping. When you wake up, the dream is gone. Enlightenment is similar to the state of waking up, and seeing things as they are. We are so afraid of so many things because we think they are real. It is like the analogy of mistaking a rope for a snake. A person walking in the dark thinks he has stepped on a snake; he is frightened and starts to run; he almost has a heart attack. But, with light, he realizes there was a mistake; it was just a rope. At no time was there a snake. The snake was only in his mind. At no time were there friends or enemies; the distinction is only in the mind. The same person whom you love quickly becomes your enemy when you change your mind. You desire something and that thing looks very good, but when you possess it, the illusion is gone. Then you chase after something else.

Happiness is our true nature. Unhappiness and negativity are unreal. There is a story of a baby lion who thought he was a sheep because he was raised by a mother sheep and lived with sheep all his life. He forgot his true nature as a lion until another lion (the Guru) came, and showed him his true nature. Then he roared like a lion instead of bleating like a lamb. Thus, knowing that in reality nothing can hurt us and that the Self is always there, we face our challenges with courage rather than weakness.

We are always complaining and crying out of attachment and desires because we have forgotten our true nature as Sat Chit Ananda.
The practice of Self Enquiry, or "Who am I?" and the practice of Discrimination (right thinking) ultimately help us to face our illusions and remove our identification with the Not-self or with our changing mind, thus realizing our true Self as Sat Chit Ananda.

Ultimately, all the Yoga practices bring us to realize our true nature and free us from the suffering that comes from identifying with our body, mind, and our ego. This is the real goal of Yoga.

CHAPTER 13

Love, Bhakti Yoga, and Gods and Goddesses

"Love is divine. Love is nectar. Love is the greatest power on earth. Love alone can transform the world. Love alone can bring peace on this earth. Love alone can conquer the hearts of others."

—Swami Sivananda

WHAT IS BHAKTI YOGA?

Swami Sivananda says in *Bliss Divine*, "Bhakti is continuity of devotion. Bhakti is attraction of the Soul to the Lord, just as there is attraction of the needle to the magnet. Bhakti is love for love's sake. There is neither selfish expectation nor fear. Bhakti is not emotionalism, but it is the tuning of the will as well as the intellect towards the Divine. It is supreme love of God. Love is natural to everybody. Bhakti is the easiest approach to God."

WHO IS GOD?

Swami Sivananda says, "God has all names and all forms and no name and no form. God exists. He is indefinable. God is the totality of all that exists, sentient and insentient. He is omnipotent, omnipresent, omniscient. He has no beginning, middle nor end. He is the indweller in all beings. He controls from within. He dwells in your heart."

Our personal relationship with the Supreme depends on our own mind. Gods and Goddesses of India represent these different manifestations of the same Supreme God. Bhakti Yoga is the path of developing a personal relationship with the personal aspect of God and consists of such practices as singing Kirtan, Puja, worshipping, prostrating, telling stories, and celebrating spiritual holy days.

The idea is to convert emotions into devotion, and to eventually realize Oneness with the Supreme through pure, selfless love.

WHAT IS LOVE?

God is love and love is God.
Swami Sivananda says, "Love is the law of life. To love is to fulfill the law. To live is to love. To love is to live. You live so that you may learn to love. You love so that you may learn to live in the Eternal. A life without faith, love and devotion is a dreary waste. It is real death.

Love of body or skin is passion. Love of God is prem. It is pure love. It is love for love's sake. Love vibrates in the form of service, charity, generosity and benevolence.

True religion does not consist of ritualistic observances and pilgrimages, etc., but in loving all. Cosmic love is all-embracing and all-inclusive. Hatred breeds hatred. Love begets love. Fear breeds fear. It is the natural right of love, the power of God, to prevail upon this earth, conquering all forces of hate and evil. Love is the hope of this dark and lonesome world. This world needs leaders filled with sympathy, cooperation, love, sacrifice, compassion, and tolerance. The saints, seers and prophets of all religions have spoken of love as the end and aim or goal of life.

Live in love. Breathe in love. Sing in love. Eat in love. Drink in love. Talk in love. Pray in love. Meditate in love. Think in love. Move in love. Die in love. Purify your thoughts, speeches and actions in the fire of love. Feel that this body is the moving temple of God. Feel that all beings are images of the Lord. Feel that one power of God works through all hands, sees through all eyes, hears through all ears. You will become a changed being. You will enjoy the highest peace and bliss."

WHY WORSHIP DIFFERENT FORMS OF GODS?

God is one, but the names are many. Truth is one, but the paths are many. At the beginning of the spiritual path, devotees superimpose God and his attributes on the name and form or idol they worship. Gradually, they begin to feel that the Lord in the idol is in the hearts of all creatures, and in all names and forms of this universe. They begin to feel His presence everywhere. The images of the deities or their names are only symbols to fix the minds of the devotees in the beginning and help them to develop concentration and one-pointed devotion. The idol is only a symbol of the divine in the same way a flag is only a symbol of a country, or a photo of a dear one is only a symbol of the love you hold towards the person.

WHAT IS ISHTA-DEVATA? WHAT IS BHAVA?

Ideally, to cultivate Bhakti you need to choose your Ishta-devata (chosen ideal or chosen form of God) and your personal relationship (Bhavas) with your Ishta.

The main Bhavas, or devotional feelings, one can cultivate are: the relationships of Master/Servant; the relationship of Teacher/Student; the relationship of Husband/Wife; the relationship of Lover/Beloved; the relationship of Mother/Child; the relationship of Father/Child; the relationship of Friend/Friend.

There are three different aspects or functions of God. God's name varies according to his function:

Creator - All things which exist must be created.

Preserver - All things which exist must be maintained or preserved for some time.

Destroyer - All things which exist must change, or be destroyed over time.

Each function has a male and female aspect, the consciousness aspect and the energy aspect respectively, which are inseparable. These are represented by the Gods and their shaktis, the Goddesses.

GODS AND GODDESSES OF INDIA

There are many names of God, because God is all names and forms, and that which is beyond names and forms. This is why in the Bhakti scriptures there are 108 or 1,008 descriptions, or names, of God. These various names detail the characteristics and glories of the different aspects of God. 108 is a sacred number, as represented by the 108 beads of the Japa mala, which is used as a tool to concentrate during mantra repetition.

The main deities:

Brahma is the creator.

Saraswati is the goddess of music, arts and wisdom.
Mantra for meditation: OM AIM SARASWATYAI NAMAH

Vishnu, the Preserver, Lord of Peace, manifests as different incarnations at various times to save mankind; Rama, Krishna and Lord Buddha are all said to be his incarnations.
Mantra for meditation: OM NAMO NARAYANAYA
Swami Vishnu-devananda promoted wide-scale repetition of this mantra for creating peace and protection in our present time.

Rama, the seventh incarnation of Lord Vishnu, is the Lord of Righteousness.
Mantra for meditation: OM SRI RAMAYA NAMAH

Krishna, the eighth incarnation of Lord Vishnu, is the Lord of Love.
Mantra for meditation: OM NAMO BHAGAVATE VASUDEVAYA

Lakshmi is the goddess of prosperity, love, virtues, health, and wealth.
Mantra for meditation: OM SRI MAHA LAKSHMYAI NAMAH

Siva is the Destroyer, the God of Transformation.
Mantra for meditation: OM NAMAH SIVAYA

Durga is the goddess of inner strength, protection and the destroyer of negativities.
Mantra for meditation: OM SRI DURGAYAI NAMAH

Ganesha is the remover of obstacles; he is the son of Siva and Parvati.
Mantra for meditation: OM SRI MAHA GANAPATAYAI NAMAH

Swami Sivananda - Satguru of our lineage
Mantra for meditation: OM NAMO BHAGAVATE SIVANANDAYA

Swami Vishnu-devananda - Guru of our lineage
Mantra for meditation: OM NAMO BHAGAVATE VISHNU-DEVANANDAYA

Your relationship to God is personal; it transcends and encompasses all human relationships. You can strengthen the relationship tremendously by the practice of repeating the divine name (Japa Yoga), the practice of chanting the divine name (Kirtan), as well as the practice of worshipping the divine form (Puja), and the practice of remembering God at all times. There are many Bhakti scriptures telling stories of devotion as well. Also, studying the lives of saints and living in their company (Satsanga) is a good and easy way to develop Bhakti.

As mentioned in the lecture on mantras (Chapter 14), mantras need to be initiated by a spiritual teacher and pronounced properly.

SWAMI VISHNU-DEVANANDA

CHAPTER 14

Mantras and Meditation

"Meditation is the only royal road to the attainment of Freedom. It is a mysterious ladder which reaches from earth to heaven, from error to truth, from darkness to light, from pain to bliss, from restlessness to abiding peace, from ignorance to knowledge, from mortality to immortality."

—Swami Sivananda in *Bliss Divine*

WHAT IS A MANTRA? WHY SANSKRIT?

Swami Sivananda says in *Japa Yoga* that, "Mantra Yoga is an exact science. By the constant thinking of mantra, one is protected and released from the round of births and deaths. A mantra is so-called because it is achieved by a mental process. The root "man" in this word mantra comes from the first syllable of that word meaning "to think", and "tra" from "trai" meaning "to protect or free" from the bondage of the phenomenal world. A mantra when constantly repeated awakens the consciousness." Swami Vishnu-devananda in his book *Meditation and Mantras* says that, "A mantra is a mystical energy encased in a sound structure."

Upon repetition of the mantras, the energy is released. Mantras are Sanskrit invocations of the Divine. Sanskrit is also known as Devanagari, or the language of the Gods. Sanskrit is not a foreign Indian language but an ancient universal language. The 50 letters of the Sanskrit alphabet are based on the pure vibrations of our chakras. By using the mantras, we create a certain pure vibration in our astral body and mind, and we purify ourselves of all our impurities and negativities. It is like washing the mind with soap made of sound.

A mantra cannot be created or tailored for an individual. It is a sound formula given to us by Rishis, or Seers, who have used the mantra to attain the highest realization. Every mantra has a seed, a Shakti (or power), a presiding deity, a specific meter, a specific wavelength, and a plug or lock. It is an exact science and needs to be studied properly under a teacher.

WHAT IS JAPA YOGA?

Japa Yoga is a method of meditation using the sound vibration of a mantra. The vibrations clear negativities. Repetition of a mantra helps make our mind strong by increasing our power of concentration. It keeps the mind focused on one pure vibration, thus counteracting the constant jumping and restlessness of the mind on many objects. One can repeat the mantra daily, verbally or mentally, at all times or at specific times. One can also use mala beads, or write the mantra.

THE PROCESS OF INITIATION INTO A MANTRA

You can choose a mantra on the basis of the sound it makes, the image of the deity which it represents, and its meaning. The mantra can also come to you through intuition. But, to really be able to benefit from it, you need to get initiation to the mantra. The process of initiation links you spiritually to the Gurus or sages and empowers your mantra with the Shakti of the Guru. During initiation, the spiritual vibration of the mantra is transmitted to the mind of the spiritual student. It is like transmitting a flame or a light from a candle that is already lit as compared to creating the fire out of rock. Initiation to the mantra has to be done by a genuine spiritual teacher who has used the mantra him or herself. Please note that a mantra cannot be created or changed just for you because all mantras came from the meditation of ancient sages who used these specific sacred sound formulas to attain the highest level realization, and who handed them down to us in the present time.

The mantra, once initiated, should not be changed and has to be repeated daily for a specific length of time. Spiritual energy needs to be renewed and reconnected. Only one-pointed dedication to the mantra will bring about the desired results.

Relationship with Guru:
The word Guru literally means "the remover of darkness." In the Sivananda organization, we follow a long lineage of teachers, ending with Swami Sivananda and Swami Vishnu-devananda.

It is important to stick to one lineage of teachers and not shop around for gurus. It is important to qualify yourself as a disciple and practice the teachings instead of looking for miracles that come from your guru. The blessing of the Gurus is important, but you have to make self effort; no one can eat for you if you are hungry—you have to eat for yourself. A mantra, once initiated, creates a link between you and the spiritual teacher; this psychic and spiritual relationship should be kept alive to really benefit you. The longer and more consistently you work with the mantra faithfully, the faster the purification will be. The teacher will initiate you when you are ready. Keep the practice of meditation and endeavor to purify yourself. Be like a piece of blank paper which is able to absorb ink, or an empty cup which is able to hold tea. In other words, you have to let go of your ego in order to receive spiritual teachings.

There are different kinds of mantras, depending on your personality and vibration, corresponding to the different aspects of deities. There are also abstract mantras with no particular form, but with meaning. God is one and not many, even though there are many deities. All genuine mantras will lead you to the same realization, but remember that they cannot be fakes, or sold, or modified. If you are attracted to one mantra more than another, it is because of your temperament or mindset, and not because one mantra is superior to the other.

three aspects of God: Brahma (Creator), Vishnu (Preserver), Destroyer or Transformer). It is the same reality that is ted by the three aspects, and you can appeal to one or the pending on which you like. God includes all three aspects, and also beyond (see the different mantras in the preceding chapter).

The role of faith:
You become what you think upon most. In Japa Yoga, Faith is the important factor for the mantra to be effective, not the intellect or ego. There is a story of a simple farmer to whom a teacher taught many mantras but he could not retain any, until the teacher gave him the mantra of "Om Buffalo." He was so attached to his buffalo that this is the only name he could remember. After some time, the teacher was ready to give him further instructions but could not find him. Arriving at his hut, the teacher called out his name and after some commotion, he replied: "O teacher, I want to see you, but I can't get out of the door, my horns are too big!" The teacher knew then that his mind was completely absorbed in the form of the buffalo, and he was then ready for initiation!

Japa Yoga is a direct path towards concentration and meditation, and it is the easiest meditation method in this time, the Kali Yuga.

> *There is a story of a genie who promised not to kill his master if the master could keep him busy. After some time his master, a woodcutter, became worried because he was running out of ideas. His Guru came to his rescue and told him to ask his genie servant to cut a tree trunk and plant it in the courtyard, and then to ask him to climb up and down the tree as his job. After some time the genie gave up, as his mind could not cope with the repetition. In the same manner, our mind is always restless and full of desires. By constant mantra repetition, our mind becomes saturated and gives up distractions, leaving us in peace. Mantra repetition is the most effective way to keep the mind under control.*

The universal mantra Om:
In the beginning of your meditation practice, you can use the universal mantra Om (or AUM), which represents the three states of consciousness: waking, dreaming, and deep sleep. The transcendent fourth state is that of pure witness of the other three states. Om is the sound of creation, the sound of Unity, a sacred universal sound that is the basis of all language. If you have not been initiated into a mantra, you can use the universal mantra Om for meditation, regardless of your religious faith.

As your mind purifies, and your connection with your spiritual path and your Gurus ripen, you can approach a spiritual teacher for initiation. The Sivananda Vedanta Center gives mantra initiation after determining if the aspirant is committed to meditation, often at the end of the one-month intensive trainings called TTC (Teachers Training Course). The course helps to tune teacher and students, and provide the preliminary purification necessary for initiation to take place. TTC is a powerful way to prepare for a lifelong practice of meditation and mantras.

THE GOAL OF MANTRA MEDITATION

The goal is to attain the transcendental state in which everything merges together. Through the medium of the vibration of mantra, the thought is purified and comes to a telepathic state, followed by the transcendental state. This transcendental state, which can be reached in meditation, is commonly called God.

CHAPTER 15

Daily Chants and Prayers

"Kirtan is singing of God's name with feeling. Such singing has a benign effect on both the physical and subtle bodies. It is an excellent method of soothing the nerves and directing the emotions to a positive goal".

–Swami Sivananda in *Bhakti Yoga*

DAILY CHANTS

Jaya Ganesha Jaya Ganesha
Jaya Ganesha Pahimaam
Sri Ganesha Sri Ganesha
Sri Ganesha Rakshamaam

"Jaya" means "hail" or "victory to"; Ganesha (the elephant-headed deity) is the remover of obstacles; Pahimaam means "save me", and Rakshamaam means "protect me".
Picture an elephant moving through the jungle; he easily removes any obstacle which may block his path. Thus, on any venture, we ask the Lord to remove all obstacles in the path.

Saravanabhava Saravanabhava
Saravanabhava Pahimaam
Subramanya Subramanya
Subramanya Rakshamaam

Saravanabhava (or Subramanya, Kartikeya, Shanmuga, or Murugan as he is also known) is the leader of the army of the gods whose job is to destroy all demons. Lord Saravanabhava drives off all evil influences (lust, anger, greed, etc.) He ensures victory in both the inner and the outer battle.

Jaya Saraswati Jaya Saraswati
Jaya Saraswati Pahimaam
Sri Saraswati Sri Saraswati
Sri Saraswati Rakshamaam

Saraswati is the patroness of the Arts and Wisdom. Invoking her name bestows intelligence, self-control, ability, and success in deep study and scholarly projects; increased intuition, mystical, and academic wisdom; love, beauty, and auspiciousness; harmony and discriminative knowledge. She inspires good will, even in the hearts of enemies, and gives success in all forms of learning.

Jaya Guru Siva Guru Hari Guru Ram
Jagad Guru Param Guru Satguru Shyam

Om Adi Guru Advaita Guru Ananda Guru Om
Chid Guru Chidgana Guru Chinmaya Guru Om

Next, the Guru is saluted. We see him as the personification and transmitter of the teaching of God in the form of Siva (the destroyer), Hari (Vishnu, the preserver), and Rama. He is the World (Jagad), Teacher, the highest (Param) Guru, who lives in the truth (Sat), the bestower of auspiciousness (Shyam). In short, we see the Guru as God.

He is beginningless (Adi) One (Advaita = without a second) Guru, the bestower of Bliss (Ananda) Knowledge Absolute (Chid), and the vanquisher of Maya (Chinmaya).

Knowledge has to come from the teacher to the student. Everyone should accept a teacher and remember that it is not actually important whether the teacher is well-known or little-known, but it is the disciple's faith in the Guru that is important. Knowledge, that is spiritual knowledge, is inherited as it were, or passed on from the spiritual preceptor to the student. When a student accepts a teacher, he will be inheriting the spiritual wealth of both. The disciple, in turn, passes on his wealth, and thus, spiritual inheritance is continued. Such knowledge cannot be gotten in books, but only by accepting a teacher who can give his help and wisdom personally.

Hare Rama Hare Rama Rama Rama Hare Hare
Hare Krishna Hare Krishna Krishna Krishna Hare Hare

This is known as "Maha Mantra" meaning "Great Mantra". It is said to be the most powerful one in this Iron Age (Kali Yuga). It is for this reason that the Mantra should always be sung in its entirety and not broken in any way. This Mantra can be chanted to help bring about peace in the world. It also brings purity to the mind and heart of the chanter.

Satguru Natha Sri Guru Natha
Jaya Guru Natha Sivananda

Sivananda Sivananda
Sivananda Satguru Devo

Salutations to Master Sivananda. Satguru = The Guru who realized the truth. Natha = Master. Deva = Divine.

Vishnu-devananda Vishnu-devananda
Vishnu-devananda Sri Guru Natha

Salutations to Swami Vishnu-devananda

Hare Rama Hare Rama Rama Rama Hare Hare
Hare Krishna Hare Krishna Krishna Krishna Hare Hare

Om Namah Sivaya (4x)

This is the Mantra of Lord Siva, the destroyer of all evil, our true Self, the primordial Yogi. This Mantra destroys all negative tendencies. Gives harmony and poise, both internal and external. Gives intuitive knowledge, integration of mind and intellect, great strength in spiritual practices. Protects one from the effects of past bad Karma.

Om Namo Narayanaya (4x)

The Mantra of Lord Vishnu (also known as Narayana) is chanted to invoke His all-pervading power of mercy and goodness. It is through His Grace that Righteousness prevails. Repetition of this Mantra confers infinite love, prosperity, power, glory, wisdom, and total liberation. It gives the ability to dissolve obstacles resulting from egoism and ignorance.

Om Namo Bhagavate Vasudevaya (2x)

The Mantra of Krishna (also called Vasudeva) is chanted to remind us of all His wonderful teachings, as Bestower of the Bhagavad Gita on mankind, etc. It grants enjoyments as well as spiritual realization, gives success in all enjoyments as well as spiritual realization, and gives success in all undertakings.

Om Namo Bhagavate Sivanandaya
Om Namo Bhagavate Satguru Nathaya

Salutations to the Divine Sivananda.
Salutations to the Divine Satguru, our Master.

Om Namo Bhagavate Vishnu-devanandaya
Om Namo Bhagavate Sri Guru Nathaya

Salutations to Swami Vishnu-devananda.

Sri Ram Jaya Ram Jaya Jaya Ram (2x)

Salutations to Rama, the seventh incarnation of Vishnu, the incarnation of righteousness and Divine conduct.

Anjaneya Anjaneya Anjaneya Pahimaam
Hanumanta Hanumanta Hanumanta Rakshamaam

Salutations to Hanuman, who is also called Anjaneya. Hanuman is the perfection of devotion. He is the greatest and the most selfless devotee of Lord Rama. He is considered to be a semi-deity, for he is the son of the wind-god. He possesses great strength and courage.

Dattatreya Dattatreya Dattatreya Pahimaam
Dattaguru Dattaguru Dattaguru Rakshamaam

Dattatreya is an incarnation of Brahma, Vishnu, and Siva. He is one of the original Gurus of Advaita Vedanta.

Sankaracharya Sankaracharya
Sankaracharya Pahimaam
Advaita Guru Advaita Guru
Advaita Guru Rakshamaam

Sankara, the great Master (Acharya), was the great propagator of Kevala (unconditional) Advaita (non-dualistic) Vedanta, and the founder of the order of Dasanami Swamis. Our lineage comes from this tradition.

Krishnam Vande Jagad Gurum Sri
Krishnam Vande Jagad Gurum

Again, Krishna is addressed as the World (Jagat) Teacher (Guru). Here we thank Him (Vande).

Anandoham Anandoham Anandambrahm Ananda
I am Bliss, I am Bliss, Bliss Absolute, Bliss I am
Om Namah Sivaya (4x)

OM TRYAMBHAKAM - MOKSHA MANTRA

MAHA MRITYUNJAYA MANTRA

The Om Tryambhakam is a life-giving Mantra. In these days, when life is very complex, accidents are an everyday affair; this Mantra wards off deaths by snakebite, lightning, motor accidents, fire, cycle, water, air accidents and accidents of all kinds. Besides, it has a great curative effect for diseases. It should be repeated before any travel.

It is also a Moksha-Mantra and bestows liberation. It is a Siva Mantra. The Mantra should be repeated 3, 9, 27 or 108 times. Especially on your birthday, repeat this Mantra as many times as possible. This will bestow on you health, long life, peace, liberation and prosperity.

Om Tryambhakam Yajamahe
Sugandhim Pushtivardhanam,
Urvarukamiva Bandhanan
Mrityor Mukshiya Maamritat

UNIVERSAL PRAYER

by Swami Sivananda

O Adorable Lord of Mercy and Love,
Salutations and prostrations unto Thee.

Thou art Omnipresent, Omnipotent and Omniscient.
Thou art Sat-chid-ananda.
Thou art Existence, Knowledge and Bliss Absolute.
Thou art the Indweller of all beings.

Grant us an understanding heart, equal vision,
Balanced mind, faith, devotion and wisdom.
Grant us inner spiritual strength to resist temptation
And to control the mind.

Free us from egoism, lust, anger, greed, hatred and jealousy.
Fill our hearts with Divine Virtues.

Let us behold Thee in all these names and forms.
Let us serve Thee in all these names and forms.
Let us ever remember Thee.
Let us ever sing Thy glories.
Let Thy name be ever on our lips.
Let us abide in Thee for ever and ever.

Om Bolo Satguru Sivananda Maharaj Ji Ki! Jaya!

Om Bolo Sri Vishnu-devananda Maharaj Ji Ki! Jaya!

ARATI

Jaya Jaya Arati Vighnavinayaka
Vighnavinayaka Sri Ganesha
Jaya Jaya Arati Subramanya
Subramanya Kartikeya
Jaya Jaya Arati Venugopala
Venugopala Venulola
Papavidura Navanita Chora
Jaya Jaya Arati Venkataramana
Venkataramana Shankataharana
Sita Rama Radheshyama
Jaya Jaya Arati Gauri Manohara
Gauri Manohara Bhavanishankara
Sambasadasiva Uma Maheshvara
Jaya Jaya Arati Raja Rajeshwari
Raja Rajeshwari Tripura Sundari
Maha Lakshmi Maha Saraswati
Maha Kali Maha Shakti
Jaya Jaya Arati Anjaneya
Anjaneya Hanumanta
Jaya Jaya Arati Dattatreya
Dattatreya Trimurti Avatara
Jaya Jaya Arati Adityaya
Adityaya Bhaskaraya
Jaya Jaya Arati Senishwaraya
Senishwaraya Bhaskaraya
Jaya Jaya Arati Sankaracharya
Sankaracharya Advaitagurave
Jaya Jaya Arati Satguru Natha
Satguru Natha Sivananda
Jaya Jaya Arati Vishnu-devananda
Vishnu-devananda Vishnu-devananda
Jaya Jaya Arati Agastya Munaye
Agastya Munaye Sri Rama Priyaye
Jaya Jaya Arati Ayyappa Swamiye
Ayyappa Swamiye Dharma Shastave
Jaya Jaya Arati Jesus Gurave Moses Gurave Buddha Gurave
Jaya Jaya Arati Mohammed Gurave Guru Nanak Gurave
Samastya Gurubhyo Namah Jaya Jaya Arati Venugopala

This is a ceremony of waving the light and chanting the names of various aspects of God as well as honoring the gurus, saints, and prophets of various religions, invoking their wisdom and light. After the chanting, we symbolically bring, with both hands, the flame towards our eyes and third eye, imbibing the light. After this, we prostrate towards the altar onto the ground, a symbolic gesture of humility and openness to receive Divine Wisdom. After prostration, the devotee receives prasad charged with the sacred energies of Arati. Prasad is an offering of sweet fruits and different foods to the Lord. Swami Sivananda says, "Don't neglect outward symbols. They are very beneficial. When viewed from the right angle or vision you will find that they play an important part in your material as well as spiritual life."

Om Na Tatra Suryo Bhati
Na Chandra Taarakam
Nema Vidyuto Bhanti Kutoyaamagnihi
Twameva Bhanta Manubhati Sarvam
Tasya Bhasa Sarvamidam Vibhati

Om Gange Cha Yamune Chaiva
Godaveri Saraswati
Narmade Sindhu Kaveri
Namastubhyam Namo Namah

Om. The sun is shining only by His grace (Brahman) and Stars and moon are shining in the night by His glory. Where will the fire stand? Fire also burns and shines because of His grace. The whole universe is standing and shining in His glory.

I prostrate and offer my prayers to the rivers Ganges, Yamuna, Godaveri and also Saraswati, Narmade, Sindhu and Kaveri. Hail to these Holy rivers.

DEDICATION SONG

Twameva Mata Cha Pita Twameva
Twameva Bandhuscha Sakha Twameva
Twameva Vidya Dravinam Twameva
Twameva Sarvam Mama Deva Dava

O God of Gods, Thou alone art my mother, father, relative, friend, learning, wealth and everything.

Kayena Vacha Manasendriyarva
Buddhyatmanava Prakriter Svabhavad
Karomi Yad Yad Sakalam Parasmai
Narayana Iti Samarpayami

Whatever actions I perform with my body, speech, mind, senses, intellect, my nature or my emotions, all these I dedicate to the Supreme Lord.

Sarva Dharman Parityajya
Mam Ekam Sharanam Vraja
Aham Tva Sarvapapebhyo
Mokshayishyami Ma Succha

Abandoning all duties, take refuge in Me (the Lord) alone, I will liberate thee from all sins, grieve not. (from Bhagavad Gita XVIII.66)

TEACHERS TRAINING COURSE CLASS AT THE SIVANANDA ASHRAM YOGA FARM

CHAPTER 16

Sivananda Approach to Yoga Postures

"Through the physical postures of Hatha Yoga,

the nervous system is toned, enabling it to withstand

the experience of rising energy. Hatha Yoga awakens

the kundalini by disciplining the body and purifying the nadis.

(The astral channels through which flows the prana)."

- Swami Vishnu-devananda in *The Complete Illustrated Book of Yoga*

THE BASIC YOGA ASANA SESSION can be from 1 to 2 hours including:

1. Beginning prayer and a short Savasana
2. Pranayama (10-15 minutes)
3. Sun salutations
4. The 12 basic asanas
5. Some additional poses and variations
   5a. An example of a properly-sequenced practice session
6. Savasana (10 minutes)
7. Ending prayers

1. BEGINNING PRAYER AND A SHORT SAVASANA

The session starts always with a few minutes of relaxation, and begins with 3 Oms, followed by prayers. The practice of prayer before the Yoga session, done mentally or verbally, helps to set the inner mood and create the proper mindset for the practice. The prayers also invoke the Gurus' and teachers' blessings for a successful practice.

2. PRANAYAMA

Pranayama can be performed before or after the session of asanas. For practical reasons, before is better. Pranayama can be performed more than one time throughout a day. 10 to 15 minutes are needed for beginners.

The two basic pranayamas are:

Kapalabhati - (shining skull—forceful breath). It is said that this pranayama cleanses the lungs and awakens energy.

Anuloma Viloma - (alternate nostril breath) It is to be done at least 10 to 20 rounds at each sitting, starting from left and ending at the left side, following the count 3-12-6 for beginners and 4-16-8 for intermediate. Use the thumb and the ring finger to hold the nostrils, and not the index finger. Keep the index finger and the middle finger turned in the palm of the right hand. Keep the sitting posture relaxed and comfortable. Keep the breathing even, following the breath, not inconsistent or too fast or too slow. This is to regulate the breath and the flow of prana. Focus throughout at the point between the eyebrows.
Rest and relax in Savasana for a few minutes after the pranayama session, enjoy the flow of energy.

3. SURYA NAMASKAR (SUN SALUTATIONS)

This is a warm-up exercise comprising 12 postures, performed continuously without a break, without variations or pauses. Each round is one full set on the left and one full set on the right The minimum is four—or better six—rounds. Every movement is accompanied by the breath. The Sun Salutations can be done slowly or fast as desired. All muscles and ligaments are exercised, preparing for the asana session.

4. THE TWELVE BASIC POSTURES

These 12 basic postures in the Sivananda system give you the full benefit of the practice session. Additional poses can be added but the basic postures MUST be included.

Headstand

Shoulderstand

Plough

Fish

Forward bend

Cobra

Locust

Bow

Half spinal twist

Crow

Hands to feet

Triangle

5. ADDITIONAL POSES

These are some of the additional poses added to the basic session according to capacity of the student and the time available. The guideline is that you need to be able to hold the basic posture for three minutes before you start the advanced poses. Please refer to the Section 5a with the sequence of the postures to know in which order to perform them.

Scorpion pose

Candle pose

Bridge pose

Wheel pose

Tortoise pose

Inclined plane pose

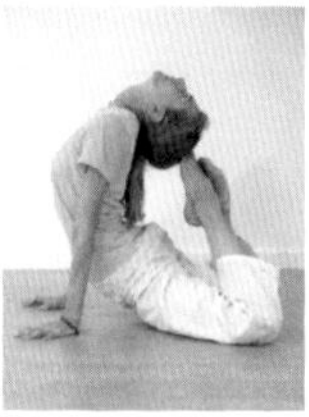

King cobra pose

Camel pose

Diamond pose

Crescent moon pose

Pigeon pose

Lotus pose

Sitting warrior pose

Cock pose

Shooting bow pose

Full split pose

Peacock pose

Tree pose

Nataraj pose

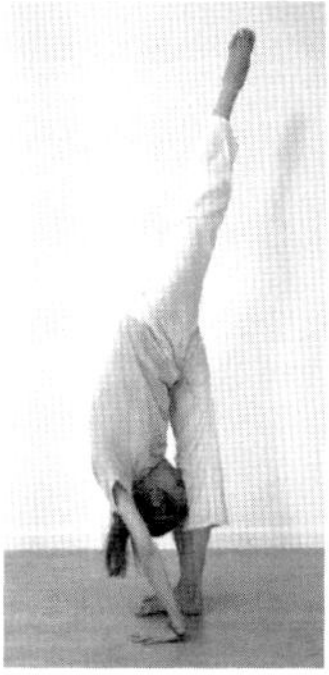

Standing split pose

Twisted triangle pose

5a. Sequence of the Postures

An example practice session and the sequence of the postures, with the twelve basic postures numbered:

1. The headstand cycle:
- Leg-raising exercises and variations
- Dolphin exercise for beginners
- Half-headstand for beginners
- Headstand (1)
- Leg variations and arm variations for advanced
- Scorpion pose for advanced

2. The shoulderstand cycle:
- Shoulderstand (2)
- Candle pose and other variations
- Plough pose (3) and variations
- Bridge pose and variations
- Wheel pose and variations
- Fish pose (4) and variations

3. The forward bend cycle:
- Full seated forward bend (5) and variations
- Tortoise pose for advanced
- Inclined plane and variations

4. The backward bend cycle:
- Cobra pose (6)
- King cobra pose for advanced
- Half locust and Locust poses (7) and variations
- Bow pose (8) and variations
- Camel pose
- Diamond pose
- Crescent moon pose
- Pigeon pose for advanced

5. The sitting cycle
- Half spinal twist (9)
- Lotus pose
- Cow face pose
- Sitting warrior pose
- Cock pose

Shooting bow pose
Leg-behind-head pose
Splits and variations for advanced

6. The balancing cycle

Crow pose (10)
Peacock pose
Handstand
Tree pose
Eagle pose
Nataraja pose
Standing forward bend (11)
Standing splits and variations for advanced
Triangle pose (12) and variations

6. FINAL SAVASANA

Lie down with legs and arms open, palms turning up. Breathe rhythmically using the abdominal breath. Systematically, tense each and every muscle from the toe to the top of the head and release them. This tension-release exercise helps the flow of prana and induces the muscle to let go of tension.

Use the mind to sweep the body from toe to head, naming consciously each and every muscle or organ, suggesting to them to relax. Allow yourself to let go of the part of the body in question, and return it to nature, releasing your identity and your attachment to it. Allow yourself to feel relaxed while resting in your subtle body.

Savasana can be performed many times a day and especially for at least 10 minutes after a Yoga session. It is the most effortless and effective method to recharge yourself physically and mentally.

7. ENDING PRAYERS

End the session with three Om trayambhakam prayers and three Om Shantihs and with pranams and praises to the teachers.

GENERAL GUIDELINES

Eat at least 2 hours before the asana session. It is difficult to perform asanas with a full stomach. Also, do not eat or drink half an hour after the session.

The best time to practice is early morning, after meditation.

Find a cool and ventilated, quiet place with an even, level floor. The best place is a space reserved for Yoga and meditation, with an altar. It is suggested not to do Yoga in the bedroom as the energy is more tamasic.

Perform the sequence of the postures in order. This will ensure the proper flow of energy.

Try to hold each posture for at least 1 to 3 minutes. It is said that holding for 3 minutes is the minimum time required to get all the benefits of the postures.

Breathe consciously during the performance of postures. When holding the posture, the breath becomes calm and the mind focused.

When holding, know where to concentrate for the specific posture.

If there is tension, focus your attention on the tension, breathe consciously while focusing on the area, sending prana to the muscles or ligaments, and during every exhalation try to progress a little more.

Yoga is not a competition, so do what you can but observe your limit. Always try to feel comfortable. Never push yourself to the point of exhaustion.

Be aware of your body throughout the session. Keep your mind focused inward and enjoy the practice.

Always relax in between the postures, with deep breathing to restore the prana and avoid fatigue.

If there is no time, stick to the basic 12 postures without variations, you will get the maximum benefit anyway.

For beginners, take the time to practice headstand by preparing your arm strength with Dolphin.

The headstand cycle goes first and the standing cycle goes last because of the spiritual principle of turning inward first to find inner balance (headstand inverts all energies, stimulating the highest chakra, going against normal tendencies, after which the energy is flowing properly) then turning the mind outward and trying to achieve balance and focus amidst worldly activities (standing postures are performed with the focus on external object to ground oneself).

The sequence of the postures follows the chakras, stimulating the chakras from the top down.

Keep the mind inspired by being aware of the physical and mental benefits of each posture.

Achieve balance through posture and counter-posture, on both the right and left sides, holding the postures on each side for an equal length of time.

If you do variations, make sure that you have time for the basic postures first. Do not skip postures.

It is better to practice in silence without music or chanting.

It is better to practice asanas with eyes closed creating an inner focus.

Do not compare or compete with each other when practicing in a group.

Group performance of asanas brings about awareness of collective energy.

It is better to practice the asanas without any props. It is a very natural way of exercising.

Use light and loose-fitting cotton clothing for better efficiency.

Use a sticky Yoga mat for better performance.

Always spend at least 10 minutes in Savasana at the end; this is the cream of the session.

To maximize the benefit of the session, keep the energy internalized and calm and do not rush right away into worldly activities.

Do not take a bath right away but allow the prana to remain for some time.

Practice daily, or at least 4 times a week, for 1 to 2 hours for maximum benefit.

BENEFITS OF PRANAYAMA AND THE TWELVE BASIC ASANAS

Kapalabhati (Cleansing Breathing Exercise)

- Cleanses the nasal passages and the entire respiratory system.
- Strengthens and increases the capacity of the lungs and the ribcage muscles.
- Helps to drain the sinuses and eliminates excess mucus.
- Removes bronchial congestion.
- Eliminates excess carbon dioxide, permitting red-blood cells to take more oxygen.
- Refreshes and invigorates the mind, increasing alertness.
- Stores prana (vital energy) in the solar plexus (navel) region.

Anuloma Viloma (Alternate Nostril Breathing)

- Cleanses and strengthens the entire respiratory system.
- Harmonizes the entire system and calms the mind.
- Increases the flow of oxygen from the lungs to the blood and enables more carbon dioxide (and other waste) to pass from the blood to the lungs for elimination during exhalation.

Surya Namaskar (The Sun Salutation)

- Makes the spine flexible. Stretches and strengthens all the major muscle groups of the body.
- Improves intake and flow of oxygen, stimulating the respiratory system and bringing increased blood flow, warmth and energy to the whole body.
- Relaxes the nerves, regulates breathing and focuses the mind.

1. **Sirshasana** (The Headstand)

- Strengthens the respiratory and circulatory systems.
- Increases oxygen supply to the brain and sympathetic nervous system, improving memory and concentration.
- Relieves pressure on the lower back and aligns the spine.
- Relieves varicose veins (as does the shoulderstand).
- Stimulates the pineal and pituitary glands.
- Counteracts nervous disorders and anxiety.

2. **Sarvangasana** (The Shoulderstand)

- Regulates the thyroid gland. Improves metabolism and heat production and proper growth of muscle and bone.
- Benefits heart rate, heart contractibility and blood pressure.
- Stimulates and regulates the parathyroid gland which helps to maintain proper calcium levels in the body.
- Keeps the neck and spine strong and elastic.
- Prevents blood from stagnating in the veins of the lower limbs.
- Removes mental sluggishness, insomnia and depression.

3. **Halasana** (The Plough)

- Increases flexibility in the neck and spine and opens up the spinal discs, rejuvenating the entire spine.
- Nourishes the spinal nerves.
- Strengthens muscles of the back, shoulders, and arms.
- Massages the internal organs.
- Relieves indigestion and constipation.

4. **Matsyasana** (The Fish)

- Removes stiffness from the entire length of the spine, bringing increased blood supply to the back.
- Corrects round shoulders.
- Increases lung capacity, strengthens and cleanses the respiratory system. Relieves asthma.
- Stimulates and massages the parathyroid glands in the back of the neck, which protect bones and teeth.
- Stimulates the pituitary and pineal glands.
- Regulates mood, emotions, and stress.

5. **Paschimothasana** (The Sitting Forward Bend)

- Stimulates digestive organs; increases digestive fire.
- Invigorates all internal organs; reduces body fat.
- Regulates the pancreas, which controls carbohydrate metabolism and blood sugar levels.
- Mobilizes joints, especially the hips.
- Invigorates the entire nervous system.
- Alleviates disorders on the genito-urinary system.

6. **Bhujangasana** (The Cobra)

- Massages and stretches deep and superficial back muscles.
- Increases flexibility of the spine.
- Relieves back pain and kyphosis.
- Tones the abdominal organs, ovaries, uterus and adrenal glands.

7. **Salabhasana** (The Locust)

- Strengthens the abdominal wall and lumbar muscles.
- Improves digestion; massages the pancreas, liver, and kidneys.
- Promotes flexibility of the cervical region of the back.
- Strengthens the biceps, deltoid muscles and back.
- Reduces lower back pain and sciatica.
- Increases space between the vertebrae.

8. **Dhanurasana** (The Bow)

- Promotes flexibility of the entire spine.
- Invigorates and massages the digestive organs.
- Alleviates constipation and indigestion.
- Regulates the pancreas.
- Strengthens the abdominal muscles.
- Prevents rheumatism of the legs, knees, and hands.

9. **Ardha Matsyendrasana** (The Half Spinal Twist)

- Keeps the spine elastic.
- Increases synovial fluid of the joints.
- Stimulates glucose release. Tones the sweat glands.
- Massages the abdominal muscles and digestive organs.
- Relieves constipation and other digestive problems.
- Tones and stimulates the sympathetic nervous system.
- Regulates the secretion of adrenaline and bile.
- Corrects stooping shoulders and poor posture.

10. **Kakasana** (The Crow)

- Strengthens and stretches the hands, arms, wrists, and shoulders.
- Increases breathing capacity.
- Increases power of concentration.
- Promotes physical and mental balance.
- Removes lethargy.

11. **Padahastasana** (The Standing Forward Bend)

- Lengthens the spine and makes it supple.
- Mobilizes the joints and invigorates the entire nervous system.
- Increases the blood supply to the brain.
- Decreases abdominal fat.
- Relieves sciatica and low back pain.

12. **Trikonasana** (The Triangle)

- Tones the spinal nerves and abdominal organs.
- Promotes hip and leg flexibility.
- Strengthens the pelvic area.
- Massages and stimulates the liver and spleen.

Savasana (The Relaxation Posture)

- Allows the body and mind to rest and recharge.
- Distributes prana throughout the body.
- Enables the benefits of the asanas to be assimilated.
- Facilitates the elimination of toxins.

CHAPTER 17

Yoga and Ayurveda

"Health is Wealth,

Peace of Mind is Happiness, Yoga shows the way."

—Swami Vishnu-devananda

WHAT IS AYURVEDA?

Ayurveda is the oldest known medical system. It is the Mother of all healing systems. It is a five-thousand-year-old Vedic Science of life, (Ayur = life, Veda = knowledge, science). Ayurveda is the traditional healing system of India, the medical side of yogic science. It includes all methods of healing from diet, herbs, exercise and lifestyle regimes to yogic practices and meditation. With its unique understanding of individual constitution, Ayurveda provides insight for each person and each culture to create a way of life in harmony with nature and one's higher Self. As Yoga is the science of spiritual development aiming at Self-realization, so Ayurveda is the science of proper living aiming to establish perfect health in body and mind.

Health: Muscle development doesn't necessarily mean a healthy body, as is commonly assumed. Health is often defined as proper functioning of all the bodily organs and systems with a general sense of well-being. Ayurveda says that health is a state of overall well-being in body, mind, and spirit which comes from living in harmony with our individual constitution and the cycles of nature around us. The Sanskrit word for health is "svastha" which means, established in the Self. When we are established in the truth of who we are, there are no symptoms of disease either in the body or the mind. Disease is defined as a lack of ease, especially related to a lack of ease of the pranic—vital life force—flow in the subtle body, which affects the mind and the physical body. Ayurveda describes that there are three energetic forces in the body, made out of the five elements: ether, air, fire, water and earth. They determine our health and also our disease. They are called the three doshas: Vata, Pitta, Kapha.

Prakruti: The Constitution

The human constitution, or Prakruti, is the inherent ideal balance of the three doshas of the body within an individual. This ideal balance is determined at conception and does not change throughout a person's lifetime. The nature of imbalance or symptoms, or Vikruti, does change. A person's constitution is an energetic force that expresses itself through their own unique genetic make-up. The three doshas determine:

- the physical and structural characteristics of our bodies.
- our internal physiological tendencies such as the level of our metabolism, and the strength of our digestive system, etc.
- our emotional tendencies and expression of our personalities.

We are healthy and can live up to our highest potential when we live according to our constitution and in rhythm with nature.

THE THREE DOSHAS OR CONSTITUTIONAL TYPES

Ayurveda recognizes three primary life-forces in the body, or three biological humors called Vata, Pitta, and Kapha, which correspond to the elements of air, fire and water. The term *dosha* literally means "that which darkens, spoils, causes harm or causes things to decay," but they only do so when functioning abnormally. When functioning normally, they maintain good health for the body and guide all the normal bodily processes.

VATA - Air and/in Ether
Dry, cold, light, mobile, subtle, rough, agitated in qualities
Vata is the biological humor of air, also translated as wind
It means that which moves things.
Governing action: movement
Chief location: large intestine (colon), pelvic cavity, bones, hips, skin, ears, thighs, nerves.
Chief symptom: pain
Other symptoms: Vata in excess causes emaciation, debility, liking of warmth, tremors, distention and constipation, as well as insomnia, sensory disorientation, incoherent speech, dizziness, confusion and depression.

PITTA - Fire and/in water
Hot, light, oily, sharp, mobile, unpleasant in odor
Pitta is the biological humor of fire, also translated as bile.
Its meaning is that which digests things.
Governing action: digestion and metabolism
Chief location: small intestine, lower stomach, blood, sweat glands, eyes, skin, liver
Chief symptom: fever
Other symptoms: Pitta in excess causes yellow color of stool, urine, eyes and skin, as well as hunger, thirst, burning sensation and difficulty sleeping.

KAPHA - Water and/in earth

Heavy, cold, moist, dull, sticky, soft, firm, gross

Kapha is the biological humor of water, also translated as phlegm.

It means that which holds things together.

Governing action: lubrication, structure and growth, stability, immune strength

Chief location: stomach, chest, throat, head, plasma, liquids of the body and synovial membranes, nose, fat, tongue, pancreas

Chief symptom: swelling.

Other symptoms: Kapha causes depression of the digestive fire, nausea, lethargy, heaviness, white color, chills, looseness of the limbs, cough, difficult breathing and excessive sleeping.

THE CAUSE OF DISEASE:

1. Forgetting our true nature as spirit
2. Unhealthy information through the sense organs
3. Misuse or under-use of the intellect
4. Decay through motion and time

Ayurvedic consultation and treatment

A key focus in Ayurveda is working on establishing a constitutionally correct diet and lifestyle. Ayurveda uses Yogic methods, like Yoga postures, breathing exercises, repetition of mantras, meditation, chanting and Yoga cleansing techniques to treat both physical and mental diseases. Ayurveda also uses treatment modalities such as the prescription of herbal formulas, and oil massages.

Ayurvedic aromatherapy, color therapy, sound therapy, and Pancha Karma cleansing and rejuvenation programs are used accordingly. The big difference between Ayurveda and Western medicine is that Ayurveda doesn't treat symptoms alone; it treats the whole person, acknowledging that each one of us is different in many ways and therefore the source of an imbalance and also the necessary form of treatment will be different.

CHAPTER 18

The Daily Sadhana Routine and Personal Strategy for Growth

"May you all become a true Jyoti (light) to lead humanity towards Peace, Light and Immortality. May you all be a true messenger of Master!"

—Swami Vishnu-devananda

WITH ALL THE BEST OF INTENTIONS, everyone wants to progress in life, and yet without knowing why, we very often find ourselves stuck. The idea is to have a strategy for our growth which is able to keep us on course and from falling victim to short-term enthusiasm.

THE FIVE ASPECTS OF THE JOURNEY

PLANTING THE TREE EXERCISE

Imagine that you are a gardener and that you are planting a tree of peace and happiness in your garden. The garden represents your mind. There are a few things you need to take care of.

1. Clearing weeds:

If your garden has not been tended for a long time, imagine that there are all kinds of weeds growing freely. If there are many weeds, you cannot really grow your tree, because the weeds will eat the nutrients in the soil and will suffocate the tree you want to plant.

Also, if your garden has not been cared for, there will be all kinds of rubbish in it. The neighbors might also have thrown garbage in it, for if the garden is not tended, it will attract disrespect.

The same is true of your mind; if you have not watched your mind and cared for the thoughts in your mind, there will be all kinds of unwanted thoughts in your mind—sexual thoughts, junk thoughts, unwanted influences of other people's thoughts, unnecessary memories and habits etc. These are weeds. They need to be cleared out before you can start your gardening work.

The nature of weeds is to grow back again after you have cleared them out. You must be patient; do not lose heart. Any bad habit that you have changed will come back again. You just have to weed again and again. Eventually what is cleared out will not grow back again. Your bad habits will disappear and you will be free of them.

Sometimes, a weed has a very deep root and you know it will take time digging to get to the bottom of the root. Some people spend their days in therapy, digging into their past. There are unending pasts, considering that we have had other lives, and that the present behaviors and fears came from a long time ago.

One helpful idea is to clear the surface of the ground, make it seem clean—even though you know that the root is still there —and carry on with your business of planting the tree. When you have time, you can come back to it and dig a little. When your tree grows, it will take over; the weed and its roots will be overpowered anyway. It cannot create harm.

Focus on building your positive life and habits starting now, and do not dwell on the past. Start your new life from today.

2. Planting the seed:

In order for your beautiful tree to grow, you need to choose a very good seed to start with. A good seed makes a powerful tree. Metaphorically, your intention to find peace, positivity and happiness for yourself needs to be pure and strong. If you ask yourself, "Do I want happiness?" everyone will say, "Yes! I definitely want happiness!" Why then do you do things that will make you miserable? The answer may be that you do not really want to be happy. So the conscious choosing of a good seed and putting the seed in the ground is a necessary step.

Some people do not really know what they want in life. They have to take the time to ask themselves the question. Lord Buddha led a good life in the palace, but when he asked himself questions, he realized that the palace life was not what he wanted, because it would not give answers to the fundamental questions he had. He realized that this life is impermanent, and he wanted to base his life on something more permanent—on the truth that would set him free. He said, sitting under the Bodhi Tree, "I am not going to budge from my seat until I am find the Truth." With that strong determination, he plunged himself into meditation and became enlightened.

Our intention to find peace and happiness needs to be strong for our efforts to bear fruits. A weak will cannot lead us very far. We need to spend time looking inward and thinking about our past mistakes and our illusions, as well as have the inner desire to be free and happy. We need to feel it very strongly. That voice has been there all the time—the desire to know, to be free, to be happy. But that voice has not been heard for a long time. It has been buried under so many other voices. We do not feel that we deserve to be Happy. We have doubt that Happiness can truly exist. We take it for granted that, "Life is what it is, imperfect. Why bother?"

Close your eyes, meditate for a moment, feel your inner voice. Dare to affirm to yourself, "I want to be happy! I want to know Peace! From now on, I will only follow this feeling that Peace exists and that I am Peace and Happiness." This is a beautiful moment; you have put the seed, the pure intention in the ground. Now it will grow...

3. Building a fence:

Your little tree is piercing through the ground and becoming a new shoot. It is in great danger of being destroyed by the elements, the children in the neighborhood, a dog, a cat.... It is imperative to protect it. You can put it in the greenhouse and transplant it later when it is stronger (go to an ashram and be protected in the beginning of your journey!) or you can build a fence around it.

What is the fence that will protect your desire for growth and allow you to grow into the beauty that you feel within? The fence is your list of weaknesses, your NOT-TO-DO list. We all have weaknesses. Our efforts to be good always get destroyed by our moments of weakness. We need to guard ourselves against them. Take the time to make an inventory of the miserable moments in your life, and make a list of those things that you should not do, as indulgence in any of the bad habits will limit your progress.

> *Example: An ex-alcoholic would have to say, "I will not drink even a drop of alcohol. I will not touch alcohol at any cost." For an emotional person, who always gets in the wrong kind of relationship and destroys him or herself, that person needs to put on the list, "I will not enter into a particular kind of relationship. I am not ready for it. Something about me needs to be strengthened before I can let someone else come in my life." For another person, it will simply be, "I will not take any sugar." For another person, it would be, "I will not depend on my family to be happy."*

You have to clearly identify those unhelpful emotional or mental tendencies. If you are attached to them, know that this is the beginning of your problem. The fence means that you will have to live without them. You have to renounce them, as they are a hindrance to your happiness, even if you are attached to them. You can reassure yourself that for now, "I should not do it." There will be a day, when you will be stronger...then maybe you can.

4. Watering and nourishing:
All plants and trees need the basic sunshine, water, and nutrients. You need to nurture yourself with good energy. Sadhana is spiritual practice that changes consciousness and the way you see things. Yoga sadhana offers you a variety of interesting and inspiring things to do for yourself. You do, however, have to find time to do them for a long period, in a regular manner. Imagine you decided to pour buckets of water on the tree you are growing because you are going away on vacation, and will not water it for months afterwards! Growth is day by day. We have to do Yoga every day because we experience stress every day. We have to eat and sleep every day, so why not take care of our spiritual growth and health every day? The key to success is regularity and realistic planning on how to

implement the good things in your present life, little by little. After all, you only have 24 hours a day and you have a life to live.

The nutrients are your program of sadhana, your conscious actions, your TO-DO list. Swami Vishnu-devananda has given us a perfect plan, a recipe for success, covering all our needs: Proper exercise (asana), Proper breathing (pranayama), Proper relaxation (Savasana), Proper diet (vegetarianism), Positive thinking and meditation (Vedanta and Dhyana).

You just have to adapt this plan to your life. How? Take a mental photograph or survey of your life as it is at this moment. Write down a list of how you typically spend your time. Maybe you can follow yourself for a week and write down what you do, how many hours you sleep, how many hours you keep company with friends, how many hours you exercise, how many hours you study, how many hours you spend alone, etc.... Now, rewrite the program of your life, adding good things to do, adjusting yourself in order to create the time for it. Balance them out

This is a sample of a beginner's daily schedule:

6–7 hours sleep (for a healthy adult, you do not need more; if you get more, you will not be happy as there is too much Tamas in your system).

1½ hour asana session including 15 minutes of pranayama and 10 minutes in Savasana.

20–30 minutes of meditation (silent meditation with the eyes closed, using a mantra, or Om, focusing internally, letting go of all concerns, at a regular time, in a regular place).

1 hour of study or self-study, alone, in contemplation, thinking about what you read, journaling, relaxing.

1–2 hours of your favorite sattvic hobby or engaging in sattvic entertainment: walking, swimming, playing music, gardening, watching a movie, dancing, etc. Make sure that what you do is not undoing your other work. For example, a film that you watch could disturb your peace of mind.

6 hours of positive work. If your work is negative then add on some hours of volunteer work for something that you feel good about. If you are working too much, you will drain yourself of prana. If you are not working at all, you will not feel good as you will feel unable to contribute and express yourself.

3 hours reserved for food: cooking, eating, and digesting. Ideally, you plan your week so that you can purchase fresh grains and vegetables and be able to cook healthy meals for yourself and your family without wasting too much time. Meals need to be healthy and not too fancy; you eat to live, not live to eat. It just takes a little planning to provide for your meals. You can create special dinners and feasts from time to time, on weekends and holidays. A good habit to adopt is to eat two full meals a day, with a light breakfast, and not to eat anything between meals.

2 hours reserved for friends and family. This depends on your situation. The idea is that if you spend too much time with friends and family, even though you might love them very much, eventually you will not be happy because you are not spending time with yourself or with things that will help you progress. Note that most of the time we spend with friends and family is not quality time. It is better that we really communicate with each other and deepen our relationships than just spend time chit- chatting without much attention. Quality of time is better than quantity of time.

2 hours for personal hygiene: laundry, bathing, housekeeping, etc...

2 hours for miscellaneous free time: transportation, etc...

Add all this together and adjust your program to your needs. You have only 24 hours a day. Swami Sivananda's formula is, "Little, little!" not a lot, then nothing. Be regular in doing a little good at a time in a balanced manner!

5. Visualizing the fruits:

If you follow this program of life, your TO-DO list, and if you stay within the fence of your NOT-TO-DO list, why then do you sometimes fail to achieve your goal? The reason for this is that you lose inspiration. This is a life of self-discipline. You might be motivated in the beginning, but for how long? Two or three months? This will not be sufficient to change deep negative habits. You will have to follow this program for a long time. How long? It is good to make your plan for a year and revise it every New Year, evaluating your progress, and feeling how different you have become, and how happy you are with yourself.

You still need, however, to deal with the lack of consistency of your mind, and the desire to resist discipline and to instead follow a happy-go-lucky life. After all, why get up early and meditate when you can sleep and indulge yourself in bed? Why refrain from eating sugar cookies and fast food when it is so available all around us? Why restrict social time when you enjoy company? You have to keep yourself motivated and inspired again and again.

This is when the last step of your strategy comes in handy. You have to visualize the fruits of your tree of Peace. Your tree will grow; you have to name the fruits that you, your family and the whole world will enjoy without doubt.

For example, you will enjoy the fruit of Health, the fruit of Love, the fruit of Freedom, the fruit of Peace and Contentment, the fruit of Self-Knowledge, the fruit of Happiness that lasts.

It is worth it after all! A little awareness, a little planning, and a little strategy is all that is needed. You must watch these five stages of your growth, and not neglect any.

Sometimes, you lose heart because it all seems so vague and unending, and you can't see the results. You just have to reassure yourself and look at yourself more carefully; you have grown a lot, and you have changed a lot—more than you can imagine. A spiritual diary is very handy as it gives you an objective view of yourself (see sample, page 119). Sometimes, you feel that you are not doing much when you are actually doing a lot, and sometimes, the opposite is true: you think a lot about doing things, but in fact you are spending little time doing them. The real truth is that the more time you spend in sadhana, the happier and more peaceful you will be.

Also if you are not balanced, or you neglect any of these stages, you will sometimes feel that you are not making progress, because what you do might be undone by yourself. If there is a hole in the fence, for example, no matter what you do, you end up feeling miserable and that you are wasting your time. You just have to close the fence and start over again.

DO IT NOW

Make a drawing of your tree now and start making your list. You can spend maybe three days thinking about it, then complete your list and try to follow it as best you can. Do not change the plan every few days. Make a plan for one month when you are beginner, make a plan for 3 months or 6 months if you are intermediate, and make a plan for one year when you are more established.

Hang your tree drawing on the wall, in a visible place so that you can be reminded at all times. Do not hide the plan from yourself; you need to face it.

If you get confused along the way, then go back to the drawing board; start again with pulling the weeds, planting the seed, building the fence, watering and nurturing the sapling, and visualizing the fruits.

Sample Spiritual Diary

	MONDAY	TUESDAY	WEDNESDAY	THURSDAY	FRIDAY	SATURDAY	SUNDAY	TOTAL
What time did you get up?								
How many hours did you sleep?								
How long did you meditate?								
How long did you do Kirtan?								
How long did you do Pranayama?								
How long did you do Asanas?								
How long studying spiritual books?								
How long in Karma Yoga?								
How long in mouna?								
How much charity given?								
How many lies told?								
How long and how often angry?								
What virtue are you developing?								
What vice are you eradicating?								
What time did you go to bed?								

Glossary

Ahimsa - non-violence

Ajna chakra - the "third eye", the spiritual energy center corresponding to the area between the eyebrows

Anahata chakra - the spiritual energy center corresponding to the heart plexus

Anuloma viloma - alternate nostril breathing, a form of pranayama

Apana vayu - the downward moving energy responsible for elimination and procreation

Aparigraha - non-acceptance of bribes, one of the five restraints in the discipline of Raja Yoga

Arati - a ceremony dedicated to the light of inner wisdom, using, symbolically, an external light

Archetypes - typical psychological category

Asana - a steady posture held for the practice of meditation in the practice of Hatha, the third limb of Raja Yoga

Ashram - a spiritual retreat and training center, a Hindu monastery

Ashtanga Yoga - the eight limbed Yoga, includes Raja Yoga, Hatha Yoga, Kundalini Yoga, Tantra Yoga, Nada Yoga, etc.

Asteya - non-covetousness or lack of jealousy, one of the five restraints in the discipline of Raja Yoga

Astral body - the subtle energetic body, including the vital energy, the mind and emotions, the intellect and the ego

Atman - the true Self

Ayurveda - the Vedic science of health and healing

Bhagavad Gita - a holy scripture of India detailing the main classical paths of Yoga through a dialogue between Lord Krishna and Arjuna

Bhakti Yoga - the path of union with God through devotion

Bhava - the inner devotional feeling

Brahmacharya - the practice of sensual and sexual control, one of the five restraints in the discipline of Raja Yoga

Brahman - absolute Consciousness, the absolute Reality that is one and indivisible, infinite and eternal, all-pervading changeless Existence, Knowledge and Bliss

Causal body - the innermost of the three bodies, which contains the seed of our karmas and desires

Chakra - the astral centers located along the Sushumna Nadi

Chitta vrittis - thought waves

Devanagari - Sanskrit, the language of the Gods

Dharana - concentration, the sixth limb of Raja Yoga

Dharma - the righteous way of living as enjoined by the sacred scriptures

Dhyana - meditation, the seventh limb of Raja Yoga

Five elements - earth, water, fire, air, ether, according to ancient Vedic thought

Guna - quality or attribute born of Nature: sattva, rajas, tamas

Guru - teacher or preceptor, one who removes darkness or ignorance

Guruparampara - the Guru-disciple lineage

Hatha Yoga - system of Yoga for gaining control over the physical body and the prana; system of asanas, pranayama, bandhas, mudras, and kriyas, ending in Samadhi

Ishta-Devata - chosen form of God; tutelary deity

Ishwara Pranidhana - self surrender and devotion to God, one of the five observances of Raja Yoga

Japa - systematic repetition of a mantra

Jiva - individual soul with ego

Jnana Yoga - the Yoga, or path, of Knowledge, the intellectual and philosophical path

Kapalabhati - a purifying form of pranayama, one of the six kriyas in Hatha Yoga

Kapha - one of the three ayurvedic constitutional types (doshas) made out of water and earth

Karma - action and consequence of action, active through the law of cause and effect, binding the jiva to samsara, the wheel of birth and death

Karma Yoga - the path of selfless action

Kirlian photography - a unique type of photography that can visually capture auras

Kirtan - singing the name and glories of God

Kriya - cleansing techniques of Hatha Yoga

Kundalini - the primordial cosmic energy located in the individual, potential psychic energy

Mahasamadhi - the time when a fully realized being leaves the physical body without having to reincarnate again

Mala - a rosary of beads for japa meditation; impurity of the mind

Manipura chakra - the spiritual energy center located at the solar plexus

Mantra - sacred syllable or series of words through repetition or reflection of which one attains perfection or realization of the Self

Maya - the illusive power of Brahman; the veiling and the projecting power of the universe

Moksha - release or liberation; this term refers particularly to liberation from the bondage of Karma and the wheel of birth and death; absolute experience

Muladhara chakra - the spiritual energy center corresponding to the base of the spine

Nadi - subtle energy channel in the astral body

Niyamas - the second limb in Raja Yoga, consisting of: internal and external purity, contentment, austerity, self-study, worship of God

Om - the pranava or the sacred syllable symbolizing Brahman

Pitta - one of the three ayurvedic constitutional types (doshas) made out of fire and water

Prakruti - the inherent ideal balance of the three doshas of the body within an individual at the moment of birth

Prana - vital energy, life breath, life force

Pranayama - regulation and control of breath, the fourth limb of Raja Yoga

Pratyahara - abstraction or withdrawal of the senses from their object, the fifth limb of Raja Yoga

Prema - divine love for God

Puja - a worship ceremony

Raja Yoga - a system of Yoga, the Royal Yoga of meditation, compiled by Patanjali Maharishi, usually referred to as Ashtanga Yoga, the Yoga of eight limbs

Rajas - one of the three aspects (gunas) or qualities of Cosmic energy, responsible for movement, action and manifested as egoistic action

Rishikesh - a holy city at the foothills of the Himalayas where Swami Sivananda lived and taught

Rishis - the seers or sages with divine wisdom

Sadhana - spiritual practice

Sadhu - a mendicant renunciate, a sannyasin

Sahasrara chakra - the crown chakra, or the ultimate center of spiritual consciousness corresponding to the top of the head

Samadhi - super-conscious state when one experiences all knowledge and joy; oneness

Sannyas - the last stage of life when spiritual renunciation is practiced

Sanskrit - language of the Gods, composed of a 50-letter alphabet, corresponding to the inner vibration of our subtle energy centers

Santosha - contentment, joy, inner peace

Sat-Chit-Ananda - Existence, Knowledge and Bliss Absolute

Satsang - association with the wise, spiritual company

Sattva - one of the three aspects (gunas) or qualities of Cosmic energy, responsible for purity, light, balance, wisdom, and goodness

Satya - truthfulness or non-lying, one of the five restraints of Raja Yoga

Saucha - purity, internal and external cleanliness, one of the five observances of Raja Yoga

Savasana - relaxation pose

Seva - selfless service in the spirit of Karma Yoga

Shakti - Cosmic divine energy

Sublimation - transformation of energy by channeling the lower emotions or desires to a higher level

Sushumna nadi - the central psychic energy channel corresponding to the spinal cord

Svastha - health, established in the Self, an Ayurvedic concept

Swadharma - one's own prescribed duty in life

Swadhisthana chakra - the spiritual energy center corresponding to the genital area

Swadhyaya - study of religious scriptures, especially the Vedas; Self-study; one of the five observances of Raja Yoga

Swamiji - respectful and devotional term to address a Swami; in the Sivananda Yoga Vedanta Centers it often refers to Swami Vishnu-devananda

Tamas - one of the three aspects (gunas) or qualities of Cosmic energy, responsible for inertia, darkness, and ignorance

Tapas - austerity, one of the five observances of Raja Yoga

Tratak - a yogic cleansing and concentration exercise consisting of staring at a flame

Vata - one of the three ayurvedic constitutional types (doshas) made out of air and ether

Vayu - vital breath, air

Vedanta - literally meaning "end of the Vedas"; the school of thought based primarily on the Upanishads; the philosophy of oneness; the ultimate end or goal of knowledge

Vedas - the revealed scripture of the Hindus containing the Upanishads

Vikruti - the state of constitutional imbalance according to Ayurveda

Vishudha Chakra - the spiritual energy center corresponding to the throat

Yamas - the first limb of Raja Yoga; ethical restraints consisting of: non-violence, non-lying, non-indulgence of senses and sexual energy, non-covetousness, non-grasping for material gain

Bibliography

The Divine Life Society. *Sivananda, Biography of a Modern Sage*. Rishikesh, India Divine Life Society, 1985.

Emoto, Masaru. *The Hidden Messages in Water*. New York, NY. Beyond Words Publishing, 2004.

International Sivananda Yoga Vedanta Centres. *Kirtan Sivananda Chantbook*. Val Morin, Quebec, International Sivananda Yoga Vedanta Centres, 1989.

International Sivananda Yoga Vedanta Centres. *Sivananda Yoga Teachers' Training Manual*. Val Morin, Quebec. International Sivananda Yoga Vedanta Centres, 1989.

Krishna, Gopala. *The Yogi: Portraits of Swami Vishnu-devananda*. St Paul, MN. Yes International Publishers, 1995.

Sivananda, Swami. *The Bhagavad Gita*. Rishikesh, India. Divine Life Society, 1939.

Sivananda, Swami. *Bhakti and Sankirtan*. Rishikesh, India. Divine Life Society, 1941.

Sivananda, Swami. *Bliss Divine*. Rishikesh, India. Divine Life Society, 1964.

Sivananda, Swami. *Elixir Divine*. Rishikesh, India. Divine Life Society, 9th ed. 1988.

Sivananda, Swami. *How to Cultivate Virtues and Eradicate Vices*. Rishikesh, India Divine Life Society, 1952.

Sivananda, Swami. *Japa Yoga*. Rishikesh, India. Divine Life Society, 12th ed. 2001.

Sivananda, Swami. *Practice of Karma Yoga*. Rishikesh, India. Divine Life Society, 5th ed. 1985.

Sivananda, Swami. *The Science of Pranayama*. Rishikesh, India. Divine Life Society, 9th ed. 1971.

Sivananda, Swami. *Thought Power*. Rishikesh, India. Divine Life Society, 10th ed. 1993.

Sivananda, Swami. *Yoga Vedanta Dictionary*. Delhi, India. Motilal Banarsidass, reprinted 1973.

Sivananda Yoga Center. *The Sivananda Companion to Yoga*. New York, NY Fireside, 2000.

Sivananda Yoga Vedanta Center. *Positive Thinking Manual*. San Francisco, CA. Sivananda Yoga Vedanta Center, 1993.

Vishnu-devananda, Swami. *The Complete Illustrated Book of Yoga*. New York, NY Julian Press, Inc., 1960.

Vishnu-devananda, Swami. *Meditation and Mantras*. New York, NY. OM Lotus Publishing Company, 1978.

Vishnu-devananda, Swami. *Sivananda Upanishad*. New York, NY. OM Lotus Publishing Inc., 1955.

ABOUT THE SIVANANDA ASHRAM YOGA FARM

The Sivananda Ashram Yoga Farm is a branch of the International Sivananda Yoga Vedanta Centres, with Headquarters located in Val Morin, Quebec, Canada. Swami Vishnu-devananda founded the ashram in 1971, on 80 acres in the beautiful Sierra-Nevada foothills, three hours North of San Francisco. Swamiji taught Teachers' Training Courses at the Yoga Farm and would visit yearly. It was his favorite place for meditation and seclusion.

One of the oldest classical ashrams in North America, the Yoga Farm has become a recognized center of classical Yogic training on the West coast, and has been renovated and expanded over the years. The concepts and teachings detailed in this book are put into daily practice in ashram life, through various programs, courses, workshops, asana classes, and community meals.

Contact Information

To register for programs, courses, or retreats, or to register as a volunteer Karma Yogi or work-study, please contact us at:
(530) 272-9322

You can find more information at **www.yogafarm.org**, or contact the ashram at **yogafarm@sivananda.org**.

Sivananda Ashram Yoga Farm
14651 Ballantree Lane
Grass Valley, CA 95949

You can learn more about our organization and a center or ashram near you at **www.sivananda.org**.

Acknowledgements

This book is the result of a series of lectures given by Swami Sitaramananda in 2007. We give thanks to the Sivananda Ashram Yoga Farm staff for their assistance in editing, and particularly to Swami Sivasankariananda for graphic design work. The asana photos are of Gayatri and Omkar, taken by Sarah Browne.

INTERNATIONAL SIVANANDA YOGA VEDANTA CENTERS

Founded in 1957 by Swami Vishnu-devananda

ASHRAMS WORLDWIDE

Sivananda Ashram Yoga Camp
673 Eighth Avenue, Val Morin
Québec, J0T 2R0, CANADA
Tel.: +1 819 322 3226
E-mail: hq@sivananda.org
www.sivananda.org/camp

Sivananda Ashram Yoga Ranch
P.O. Box 195, Woodbourne, NY 12788, USA
Tel.: +1 845 436 64 92
E-mail: yogaranch@sivananda.org
www.sivanandayogaranch.org

Sivananda Ashram Yoga Retreat
P.O. Box N7550
Paradise Island, Nassau, BAHAMAS
Tel.: 242 363 29 02
E-mail: nassau@sivananda.org
www.sivanandabahamas.org

Sivananda Vrindavan Ashram Yoga Farm
14651 Ballantree Lane, Grass Valley, CA 95949, USA
Tel: 530 272 9322
E-mail: yogafarm@sivananda.org
www.sivananda.org/yogafarm

Sivananda Dhanwanthari Ashram
Neyyar Dam
P.O. Thiruvananthapuram District, Kerala 695 572 S. INDIA
Tel 1: +91-471-227-3093
Tel 2: +91 471-227-2703
E-mail: yogaindia@sivananda.org
www.sivananda.org/neyyardam

Sivananda Yoga Vedanta Meenakshi Ashram
Kalloothu, Saramthamgi Village Vellayampatti
P.O. Palamedu (Via), Madurai Dist 625 503
Tamil Nadu, INDIA,
Tel: +91 (0)94421 90661/2
E-mail: madurai@sivananda.org
www.sivananda.org/madurai/

Sivananda Kutir (near Siror Bridge)
P.O. Netala, Uttara Kashi Dt, Himalayas, U.P. 249 193, INDIA
Tel: +91.1374.22624
E-mail: himalayas@sivananda.org
www.sivananda.org/uttarkashi/

Ashram du Yoga Sivananda
26 Impasse du Bignon 45170 Neuville aux bois, France
Tel: 33 (0)2 38 91 88 82
E-mail: orleans@sivananda.org
www.sivananda.org/orleans/

International Sivananda Yoga
Retreat House (Seminarhaus)
Reith bei Kitzbühel, Bichlach 40, 6370 Reith bei Kitzbühel Tirol, Österreich
Tel: +43 5356 67404
E-mail: tyrol@sivananda.org
www.sivananda.org/tyrol

Sivananda Yoga Vietnam Resort
and Training Center
K'Lan Resort, nearby Tuyen Lam lake,
Da Lat, Vietnam
Tel: 063 650 1100
E-mail: vietnamyogaresort@sivananda.org
www.sivanandayogavietnam.org

Sivananda Yoga Vedanta Tapaswini Ashram
Guthavaripalem, Kadivedu P.O.
Chilakur Mandalam 524410, Gudur
Nellore DT., Andhra Pradesh, India
Tel: +91.8624 255577
E-mail: gudur@sivananda.org
www.sivananda.org/gudur

CENTERS WORLDWIDE

ARGENTINA

Centro Internacional Yoga Sivananda
Sánchez de Bustamante 2372,
Capital Federal-1425 Buenos Aires
Tel: +54 (11) 4804 7813
E-mail: buenosaires@sivananda.org
www.sivananda.org/buenosaires

Centro de Yoga Sivananda
Rioja 425, 8300 Neuquén
Tel: +54-29-9442-5565
E-mail: neuquen@sivananda.org

AUSTRIA
Sivananda Yoga Vedanta Zentrum
Prinz Eugen-Str. 18, Vienna 1040
Tel: +43-1-586-34-53
E-mail: vienna@sivananda.net
www.sivananda.org/vienna

BRAZIL
Centro Sivananda de Yoga Vedanta
Rua Santo Antonio 374, Bairro Independencia,
Porto Alegre 90220-010-RS
Tel: +55-51-3024-7717, Mob: +55-5198187-2422
E-mail: portoalegre@sivananda.org
www.sivananda.org/portoalegre

Centrou International Sivananda de Yoga e Vedanta
Rua Girassol 1088, Vila Madalena,
Sao Paulo - CEP 05433-002
Tel: +55-51-3032-8925, Mob: +55-11-953197175
E-mail: saopaulo@sivananda.org
www.sivananda.org/saopaulo

CANADA
Sivananda Yoga Vedanta Center
5178 St. Laurent Blvd., Montreal, Quebec,
H2T 1R8
Tel: +1(514) 279-3545
E-mail: montreal@sivananda.org
www.sivananda.org/montreal

Sivananda Yoga Vedanta Center
77 Harbord St.,Toronto, Ontario M5S 1G4
Tel: +1(416) 966-9642
E-mail: toronto@sivananda.org
www.sivananda.org/toronto

FRANCE
Centre Sivananda de Yoga Vedanta
140 rue du Faubourg Saint-Martin,
75010, Paris
Tel: +33-1-40-26-77-49
E-mail: paris@sivananda.net
www.sivananda.org/paris

GERMANY
Sivananda Yoga Vedanta Zentrum
Schmiljanstrasse. 24, D-12161 Berlin
Tel: +49-30-85-99-97-98
E-mail: berlin@sivananda.net
www.sivananda.org/berlin

Sivananda Yoga Vedanta Zentrum
Steinheilstrasse1/ Luisenstrasse 45,
D-80333 Munich
Tel: +49-89-700-9669-0
E-mail: munich@sivananda.net
www.sivananda.org/munich

INDIA
Trivandrum - India
Sivananda Yoga Vedanta Center
TC 37/1927 (5), Airport Road West Fort PO,
Thiruvananthapuram 695023, Kerela
Tel: +91-471-245-0942, Mob: +91 9497008432
E-mail: trivandrum@sivananda.org
www.sivananda.org/trivandrum

Sivananda Yoga Vedanta Nataraja Center
A41, Kailash Colony, New Delhi 110048
Tel: +91-11-4059-1221, +91-11-2924-0869
Mob: +91 8860954455
E-mail: delhi@sivananda.org
www.sivananda.org/delhi

Sivananda Yoga Vedanta Dwarka Center
PSP Pocket, Sector-6 (near DAV school, next to Kamakshi Apts), Swami Sivananda Marg,
Dwarka 110075
Tel: +91-11-6456-8526, +91-11-4556-6015/6
E-mail: dwarka@sivananda.org
www.sivananda.org/dwarka

Sivananda Yoga Vedanta Center
3/655 (Plot No. 131), Kaveri Nagar Kuppam Road, Kottivakkam, Chennai 600 041
Tel: +91-44-2451-1626, +91-44-2451-2546
E-mail: chennai@sivananda.org
www.sivananda.org/chennai

Sivananda Yoga Vedanta Center
444, K.K.Nagar, East 9th Street
Madurai 625020, Tamil Nadu
Tel: +91-0452-2581170, +91-0452-4393445
Mob: +91 9092240702
E-mail: maduraicentre@sivananda.org
www.sivananda.org/maduraicentre

ISRAEL
Sivananda Yoga Vedanta Center
6 Lateris St., Tel Aviv 64166
Tel: +972-3-6916793
E-mail: telaviv@sivananda.org
www.sivananda.co.il

ITALY
Centro Yoga Vedanta Sivananda Roma
Via Oreste Tommasini, 7, Roma 00162
Tel: +39-06-94326556, Mob: +39 3474261345
E-mail: roma@sivananda.org
www.sivananda-yoga-roma.it

JAPAN
Sivananda Yoga Vedanta Centre
4-15-3 Koenji-Kita, Suginami-ku,
Tokyo 1660002
Tel: +81 03-5356-7791
E-mail: tokyo@sivananda.org
www.sivananda.jp

LITHUANIA
Sivananda Jogos Vedantos Centras
M.K. Ciurlionio g. 66, Vilnius 03100
Tel: +370-864-8728-64
E-mail: vilnius@sivananda.ne
www.sivananda.org/vilnius

SPAIN
Centro de Yoga Sivananda Vedanta
Calle Eraso 4, Madrid 28028
Tel: +34-91-361-51-50
E-mail: madrid@sivananda.net
Web: www.sivananda.org/madrid

SWITZERLAND
Centre Sivananda de Yoga Vedanta
1 Rue des Minoteries, Geneva 1205
Tel: +41-22-328-03-28
E-mail: geneva@sivananda.net
www.sivananda.org/geneva

UNITED KINGDOM
Sivananda Yoga Vedanta Center
45-51 Felsham Rd.,London SW15 1AZ
Tel: +44-20-8780-0160
E-mail: london@sivananda.net
www.sivanandalondon.org

UNITED STATES OF AMERICA
Sivananda Yoga Vedanta Center
1246 West Bryn Mawr, Chicago, IL 60660
Tel: +1(773) 878-7771
E-mail: chicago@sivananda.org
www.sivanandachicago.org

Sivananda Yoga Vedanta Center
13325 Beach Avenue, Marina del Rey, CA 90292
Tel: +1(310) 822-9642
E-mail: losangeles@sivananda.org
www.sivanandala.org

Sivananda Yoga Vedanta Center
243 West 24th Street, New York, NY 10011
Tel: +1(212) 255-4560
E-mail: newyork@sivananda.org
www.sivanandanyc.org

Sivananda Yoga Vedanta Center
1185 Vicente Street., San Francisco, CA 94116
Tel: +1(415) 681-2731
E-mail: sanfrancisco@sivananda.org
www.sivanandasf.org

URUGUAY
Asociacion de Yoga Sivananda
Acevedo Diaz 1523, Montevideo 11200
Tel: +598 2401-0929/6685
E-mail: montevideo@sivananda.org
www.sivananda.org/montevideo

VIETNAM
Sivananda Yoga Vedanta Center
34 Suong Nguyet Anh Street, Dalat
Tel: +84 63-650-1900
E-mail: dalat@sivananda.org
www.sivanandayogavietnam.org

Sivananda Yoga Vedanta Centre
25 Tran Quy Khoach Street, District 1,
Ho Chi Minh City
Tel: +84 6680-5427, +84 6680-5428
E-mail: hochiminh@sivananda.org
www.sivanandayogavietnam.org

Sivananda Yoga Vedanta Center
Fengge Yayuan 8-3-10, No. 1 Xinxiwang Road,
Wuhou District, Chengdu, Sichaun 610042
Tel: +86 028-8625-7086
E-mail: china@sivananda.org
www.sivanandayogachina.org

Printed in Great Britain
by Amazon

45895931R00076